A Vindication

OF

The Catholic Church.

A VINDICATION

OF

The Catholic Church,

IN A

SERIES OF LETTERS

ADDRESSED TO

THE RT. REV. JOHN HENRY HOPKINS,

PROTESTANT EPISCOPAL BISHOP OF VERMONT.

BY

FRANCIS PATRICK KENRICK,

ARCHBISHOP OF BALTIMORE.

"Tacere ultra non oportet, ne jam non verecundiæ, sed diffidentiæ esse incipiat quod tacemus, et dum criminationes falsas contemnimus refutare, videamur crimen agnoscere."—S. Cyprian. L. ad Demetrianum.

BALTIMORE:

PUBLISHED BY JOHN MURPHY & CO.

No. 178 MARKET STREET.

PITTSBURG—GEORGE QUIGLEY.

Sold by the Principal Catholic Booksellers.

1855.

Preface.

THE following pages have been hastily written in reply to the late work of the Protestant Episcopal Bishop of Vermont, styled "The End of Controversy Controverted." The letters of which it is composed are addressed to me, and a special challenge to refute them is given, towards the end, in these words: "I commit the care of Dr. Milner's reputation to you, as his special admirer and friend." Yet I should not have noticed them, could I hope that the work of Dr. Milner would be perused generally by those who read the letters of Dr. Hopkins; for I have entire confidence that every intelligent reader must feel that the Catholic controvertist is immeasurably superior in argument, and authorities, as well as style. At this time of public excitement, I desired to remain silent, if it could be without detriment to the interests of truth; but from the air of triumph assumed by Dr. Hopkins, and the plaudits with which his work has been received by the Church Review, and other periodicals of his communion, I was persuaded that silence would be misconstrued. "I could not then remain silent any longer," to borrow the words of St. Cyprian, which I have chosen for my motto, "lest my silence should be ascribed, not to a love of peace, but to a distrust of the merits of my cause; and lest my disregard of false charges should be construed into an avowal of their truth."* In repelling his attack, I have been forced to make statements which may prove painful to the Religious denomination, in which he holds so distinguished a position; but as I give unquestionable authority for the facts, I feel justified by the necessity imposed on me, for bringing them forward. None are more willing than Catholics to bury in oblivion whatever is odious in the legislation

* L. ad Demetrianum.

or history of past ages, and to live in harmony and peace with their fellow-citizens in all the relations of life. We hold the maxim of St. Augustin: "Love the men, destroy the errors; be bold without pride in the maintenance of truth; strive for the truth without harshness; pray for those whom you rebuke and confound."*

* Contra lit. Petiliani, l. i. sub finem.

ERRATA.

Page 43. For δέος, read θέος.

48, 1st line. For "Lexrins," read "Lerins."

58. For "When this magnet," &c., read: "This is our compass, for want of which others are tossed," &c.

126, 6th line from bottom. For "antiquity," read "ambiguity."

Table of Contents.

LETTER I.

ORIGIN OF THE CONTROVERSY.

LETTER II.

RULE OF FAITH.

B

LETTER III.

ON THE SCRIPTURE.

LETTER IV.

INTERPRETATION OF SCRIPTURE.

LETTER V.

ON THE SACRAMENTS.

LETTER VI.

ON TRANSUBSTANTIATION.

LETTER VII.

ON THE SACRIFICE.

LETTER VIII.

ON COMMUNION UNDER ONE KIND.

LETTER IX.

ON PENANCE.

LETTER X.

ON PURGATORY.

LETTER XI.

ON INDULGENCES.

LETTER XII.

ON DEVOTION TO THE BLESSED VIRGIN.

LETTER XIII.

ON THE INVOCATION OF THE SAINTS.

LETTER XIV.

ON RELICS.

LETTER XV.

ON IMAGES.

LETTER XVI.

ON THE PRIMACY.

LETTER XVII.

ON TEMPORAL POWER.

LETTER XVIII.

ON ABUSES.

LETTER XIX.

ON PERSECUTION.

LETTER XX.

ON HENRY VIII.

LETTER XXI.

ON CRANMER.

LETTER XXII.

ON THE CHURCH OF ENGLAND.

LETTER XXIII.

ON THE CATHOLIC CHURCH.

VINDICATION OF THE CATHOLIC CHURCH.

LETTER I.

On the Origin of this Controversy.

Right Reverend Sir:

MORE than seventeen years have passed away since I had the honor of addressing you a series of letters, "On the Primacy of the Apostolic See, and the Authority of General Councils," in reply to your work comparing "The Church of Rome at the present day, with The Church of Rome in its Primitive Purity." As you had addressed "the Roman hierarchy," in behalf of Christian unity, urging us to discard our distinctive tenets, I felt authorized to review your book, and vindicate the claims which we recognize in our head, and in the general councils of bishops. You did not think proper to publish any rejoinder. In 1841, I imitated your zeal for unity, by writing a short letter to the Protestant Episcopal Bishops, inviting them to follow up to its legitimate consequences the movement towards the Catholic Church which had begun in England. At length, in 1843, you addressed me in a chivalrous spirit, challenging me to a public discussion of all the points at issue between our respective communions, and allowing me to bring with me to the encounter as many of my colleagues as I chose. I declined this trial of strength as undignified and unsatisfactory, but offered to open a correspondence with you on the various questions, through the columns of the Catholic Herald and New York Churchman. This proposition was not agreeable to you, so that you broke off the correspondence, intimating, however, that you would treat the matters of controversy in books, to be published at your convenience. On the refusal of the former Protestant diocesan of Philadelphia to allow you to deliver in the churches of that city "Lectures on the British Reformation," you gave them through the press as "intended to be delivered." Of these I did not feel bound to take any notice, as they had no reference to me, or my work on the Primacy. When Dr. Ives, the Protestant Episcopal Bishop of North Carolina, who has since passed to our communion, was engaged in recommending the practice of confession, you published "A History of the Confessional," with a view to counteract his dangerous tendencies and influence. This also did not concern me. In the mean time I published two editions of my work, which I divested of its epistolary form, and of all direct reference to you, enlarging it so as to serve as a general treatise on the Primacy. You and I thus appeared to have bid each other adieu, though, as you justly suppose, I had not forgotten you, and you evince by your late book that you have not forgotten me. (Manet alta mente repostum.) I was somewhat surprised, on my late return from Rome, after a short absence, to learn that you had addressed to me a series of letters, filling two large volumes, and purporting to be a review of Milner's End of Controversy. My recommendation of this work in my letter to the Protestant Bishops as calculated to place before them the main points at issue with their proofs, induced the late Dr. Samuel Farmar Jarvis, some years ago, to undertake to answer it; but his failure is manifest from the fact, that you have chosen the same arduous task, as if nothing had been attempted. He, indeed, interpreting the Apocalypse, ventured to calculate the overthrow of the Papacy, in the year in which he was writing (1847), whilst you, more wisely, avow your conviction, that it will continue until the second advent of our Redeemer. You call my attention to the fact that my recommendation did not pass unheeded; which is certainly gratifying, especially as it has taken so many years to prepare your elaborate reply. You remind me, likewise, of my anticipations, that "numbers would break from your ranks," in case you and your colleagues hesitated to join our communion, and you insinuate that I must feel mortified and disappointed, although you acknowledge that more than a dozen clergymen of the United States, with a Bishop at their head, have passed over to us, whilst in England more than a hundred, among whom are two archdeacons, of high learning and character, have abjured the Queen's supremacy. Besides, many respectable laymen, some of them in your immediate neighborhood, have followed these examples. To counterbalance these defections, you boast of sixty thousand Irish Catholics that have embraced the religion of the crown; but I fear that you have been deceived by some interested parties, whose exaggerations were directed to obtain new supplies from their patrons, in order to furnish the converts with soup, and other aids for the diffusion of their tenets.

The number of emigrants, or their descendants, who you suppose are lost to the Church in this country, is greatly overcalculated, for a case of formal apostacy is extremely rare, and many who for years neglect all practices of religious duty, are often regained with their whole families. Indeed, if the defections were numerous, the alarm which is now excited in regard to our increase, would be altogether void of pretext, and you would have no occasion to join in the hue and cry which is raised against us, or to point to our principles as perilous to the safety of the country. You might rather assume the more amiable character of pacificator, and implore the public to wait with patience, since we should soon disappear from the land under the less violent process of dissolution or amalgamation. But you are alarmed that men of high position and distinguished intelligence should pass over to us, even at the sacrifice of every worldly interest, and you feel that in the changes which take place, the advantages are greatly on our side; whence you abandon calm discussion, and appeal to vulgar prejudice. At a moment when we are likely to fall victims to a vast conspiracy against the common liberties of the country, which are assailed in us, you reappear on the field, and join in the general onslaught. The tone of your former work was courteous, almost to affectation; the select topics of which you treated, were supported with a show of learning and argument; but your controversial tactics have undergone an unhappy change. The same professions of kindliness are, indeed, repeated with increased solemnity; the same attempt is made to sustain your positions by a display of authorities; but, for the most part, you rely on the scandals and abuses of past ages, to discredit and disgrace the Church, and you meet the learned statements and reasoning of Dr. Milner by abusive epithets, and unwarranted imputations. On reading your letters, I determined not to give any special reply to them, but to refer to them in the preface and notes to a fourth stereotyped edition of my work on the Primacy, which was then in press, and which anticipated most of your charges. As, however, my manuscript arrived too late at the office, the plates being already finished, I am induced to answer briefly the chief points which you have brought under discussion, but still beg to refer to my larger treatise. Although I cannot complain of any gross violation of personal courtesy, your raillery being pardonable in a struggling controvertist, your charges are so gross and groundless, that in refuting them I may appear wanting in respect; yet I trust that I shall not forget what is due to your position, as well as my own, and to the interests of truth, which are best maintained when charity is not violated. "When I am under the necessity of answering others verbally, or in writing, even should I have been provoked by insulting charges, I endeavor, as far as the Lord gives me grace, to restrain and repress my feelings of indignation, that I may edify the hearers or readers, so that I seek not to prove superior to my adversary in railing, but profitable to others by exposing error."* St. Augustin is my guide and model.

* Contra litteras Petiliani, l. iii. n. 1.

LETTER II.

On the Rule of Faith.

RIGHT REVEREND SIR:

YOU accept the qualifications of the Rule of Faith, as laid down by Dr. Milner, namely, that it must be certain, secure, and universal. For the Church of England you claim that she is distinguished from fanatics, who take the Bible for their guide, interpreting it according to their fancy, whilst she holds the interpretation given of it by the ancient church, as embodied in the formularies, called symbols, and in the truly general councils. You do not, however, confine it to these, since you refer to the Book of Common Prayer generally, and to the Thirty-Nine Articles in particular, as exponents of the primitive doctrine. Yet as these articles were adopted only under Elizabeth, instead of the forty-two articles approved by Edward, I do not see how they can serve as sure guides to the primitive interpretation of Scripture. Besides, you blame us for doctrinal definitions made in the Council of Trent, which you brand as additions to the ancient symbols, sanctioned by the early councils: how, then, justify the English convocation or parliament in setting forth so many points of doctrine not specified in the ancient formularies? But be this as you please, you are entitled to the full benefit of the Articles and Prayer Book. It is for you to show that they so qualify and determine the interpretation of Scripture, that your members are not exposed to the danger of mistaking their own imaginations for the true meaning of the text. Dr. Milner insists that you must come down to the level of the Protestant masses from the vantage-ground which you proudly occupy: since, although you profess to understand the Scripture in conformity with the Articles, you have no certain means of determining the meaning of these, wherever they are open to ambiguity, whence the same conflict of views is witnessed among you, as in other Protestant communities.

As you refer to the ancient creeds, it may be fair to ask you, on what ground you assign them such high authority to determine the meaning of Scripture? The origin of the simplest form, called the Apostles' Creed, is a matter of question among critics, who likewise dispute as to its correct reading. Its authority must entirely rest on its ancient usage in the church. The Nicene Creed is a fuller development of it, made with a view to exclude the errors of Arius and Macedonius, by authority of the Councils of Nice and Constantinople. If their right to enlarge the ancient formulary be admitted, can it be consistently maintained that councils of bishops do not still enjoy the same power? Of the creed called the Athanasian, which contains a still clearer exposition of the mysteries of the Trinity and Incarnation, together with a declaration of the necessity of holding the Catholic faith, under pain of eternal damnation, the Church of England professes that it, as well as the other two, "ought thoroughly to be received and believed, for they may be proved by most certain warrants of Holy Scripture:" whilst Episcopalians, in the United States, have expunged it altogether from their Prayer Book, and even left it free to omit the article of the Apostles' Creed: "He descended into hell."

You speak of the great doctrines of the Gospel Faith, embodied in the primitive creeds, as derived from the Scriptures; but you must be aware that the first formulary was not the result of Scriptural examination, but a simple profession of the leading mysteries traditionally preserved from the earliest period. Although it may not be demonstrable that the apostles composed it, its chief articles were certainly professed almost in the same words, throughout all the church, antecedently, as is probable, to the writing of several books of the New Testament. They bear no appearance of being framed after the perusal of the sacred books. Dr. Nevin observes: "The creed does not spring from the

Bible. This is plain from its history. Its main substance was in use before the New Testament was formed. Peter's confession, 'Thou art the Christ, the Son of the living God,' had no such origin. It was produced from the living sense of Christ's presence itself. And so we may say, the whole creed, which lies involved in that confession, is derived through faith, out of the same living ground. It is, of course, in harmony with the Bible; for it has to do immediately with its central revelation, the mystery of the Word made Flesh. It comes not, however, circuitously, in the way of reflection and study, through its pages. The early church got it not from the Bible. Strange that there should be any confusion in regard to what is in itself so palpable and clear. The Bible is not the *principle* of Christianity; nor yet the *rock* on which the church is built. It never claims this character, and it can be no better than idolatry and superstition to worship it in any such view."* Yet you, Right Reverend Sir, gravely speak of "the Scriptural Creed," as if its very words were contained in the sacred volume.

In addition to the ancient symbols, you refer to the Thirty-nine Articles adopted by the English Convocation under Elizabeth, and by the Protestant Episcopal Convention in America in 1801, with some very serious modifications. Of

* Mercersburg Review, July, 1849, Article, The Apostles' Creed.

them you say: "There is not a single topic decided by the councils and the fathers, in the pure and primitive ages of the Church, which is not here distinctly set forth with the most admirable exactness and precision, leaving no room for heretical private judgment in any important point of Christian doctrine."* The first difficulty is, what can determine the individual member of your communion, to give the unqualified assent of his mind to the Articles themselves? Are they recommended to him by an authority which cannot err? Does he rely on the testimony and judgment of the English Parliament, or Convocation, or of the American Convention? If he must first satisfy himself, by personal examination, that the Articles express the doctrines of the early Church, the inquiry will be tedious, and the result doubtful. What must determine him to receive the decisions of the Church in those early ages with entire deference, if the Church at the present time has no claim on the unreserved assent of his mind? Truly, there is much room for private judgment on all those points, as long as an infallible authority is not claimed and exercised. Besides, few find the Articles themselves so clear and definite as you represent them, which is the cause of the existence of two great divisions among you, the High and Low Church divines, whose dif-

* Vol. 1, p. 15.

ference of views regards points of great importance. The Articles are generally considered as directing the individual judgment, rather than determining it, which is impossible, for the want of adequate authority. They are not regarded by the very ministers who subscribe to them, as binding them to assent, but rather as points to be respected in their public teaching, and have been styled, not improperly, *Articles of Peace.* Paley observes: "They who contend that nothing less can justify subscription to the Thirty-nine Articles, than the actual belief of each and every separate proposition contained in them, must suppose that the legislature expected the consent of ten thousand men, and that in perpetual succession, not to one controverted proposition, but to many hundreds. It is difficult to conceive how this could have been expected by any, who observed the incurable diversity of human opinion upon all subjects short of demonstration."* In order effectually to control Scriptural interpretation, they must be supported by some authority better than an English Act of Parliament, and there must be some tribunal to determine their meaning. The Church of England claims, indeed, "authority in controversies of faith," but she nullifies her claim, by avowing her liability to err in her decision. Thus the guidance on which you rely is unsatisfactory, and you are left, like other Protestants,

* Philosophy, Book III. Chap. 22.

with the Bible alone, to interpret it as you judge proper.

The individual is placed above the Church in the very article in which her authority is affirmed: "yet it is not lawful for the Church to ordain anything that is contrary to God's word written; neither may it so expound one place of Scripture, that it be repugnant to another." This presumes that the Church is capable of abusing her authority, by commanding what is opposed to the Scripture, and by expounding the text so as to involve contradiction. The individual must necessarily judge for himself, whether she has in fact so erred. He must examine and compare the texts, in order to satisfy himself that she has not abused her authority.

You have no reason, then, to find fault with Dr. Milner, for saying that your rule is the Bible, as interpreted by each reader for himself, since you say the same in substance: "On this ground we stand, and we ask no other. The Scriptures as the Rule of Faith, according to the *primitive Catholic interpretation*, with the right of private judgment, in order to decide *what that interpretation was*."* I fancy I hear some citizen whose principles have been represented as inconsistent with law and order, inasmuch as he professes to respect the laws only as far as he understands them, without reference to the authority of the

* Vol. 1, p. 286.

legal tribunals. He repels the imputation as groundless, because he accepts them as they were expounded by the judges soon after their enactment; but he insists that he must be allowed to determine for himself what their decisions were, and how far they are applicable to his circumstances. By claiming for the individual the right to determine for himself, what was the primitive Catholic interpretation, you give him indirectly the right to determine the meaning of the sacred text itself, and thus fall back on the common ground of Protestants, the Bible as interpreted by each one's private judgment.

In truth you have no doctrinal tribunal which can exercise this authority, claimed in the Articles. In England, the whole Church authority is concentrated in the Queen and Privy Council, who seem disposed to leave questions open rather than to decide them, as was seen in the Gorham case regarding baptismal regeneration. In this country the General Convention is your highest tribunal, which, I presume, may at most censure some individual for teaching erroneous doctrines, contrary to the pledges given at his ordination. In such a case the symbols and Articles would naturally be referred to, and their obvious meaning insisted on; but as many controversies have been raised on them, no decision in any special case is likely to be given or to obtain weight so as to fix the meaning beyond dispute. You have then, practically, no rule of faith beyond the Presbyterians, Methodists, or other sectaries, who claim and exercise a similar right over their preachers, suspending or dismissing them for teaching doctrines opposed to their confessions of faith. This exercise of authority is merely disciplinary, not capable of determining the assent of the mind, since it emanates from a tribunal confessedly liable to err. The Articles may serve as guides to influence and direct the judgment of the individual, and as rules by which to try and judge him, in case his teaching be deemed erroneous; but they altogether fail in that which is essential to a rule of faith, which is, to determine the revealed doctrines, so that they may be accepted and held with entire certainty.

In confining the rule of faith to the ancient symbols or to the Thirty-nine Articles, you leave without protection all the revealed doctrines which are not formally embraced and specified in them. Any truth recorded in the Sacred Scriptures ought certainly to be received with the homage of our understanding; yet it may not be directly stated in those formularies. If the Church can only point to them, without venturing beyond their specifications, her authority as the witness of revealed doctrine becomes null in all cases of this character. In all cases whatsoever it is necessarily null as regards the assent of the mind, which it cannot claim, unless it has a divine assurance of infallibility.

You are most unfortunate, Right Reverend Sir, in referring to the Council of Chalcedon as forbidding any symbol of faith, or definition of doctrine beyond the formulary which is called the Nicene Creed. These fathers were, indeed, for a time indisposed towards the adoption of any new formulary; but finding that certain Egyptian monks, infected with the Eutychian heresy, made no difficulty in assenting to the symbol of Nice, they deemed it necessary to exact of them a fuller profession of faith, directly opposed to the error of which they were suspected. Accordingly they drew up a decree, in which they accepted, in the first instance, the Nicene Creed, with the additions made by the Council of Constantinople, to exclude the heresy of Macedonius. They begin by remarking that "the wise and salutary symbol of divine grace (the Nicene symbol) was sufficient for the knowledge and confirmation of piety; but since those who endeavor to reject the preaching of truth, have invented new terms, according to their respective heresies, on this account this present holy, great, and universal synod, wishing to close against them all devices against the truth, teaching this doctrine which is immovable from the beginning, has decreed before all things that the faith of the three hundred and eighteen holy fathers should remain entire and inviolate." In like manner they approved the synodical letter of St. Cyril of Alexandria, to which the fathers of

Ephesus had assented, as a correct exponent of the symbol, and an antidote against the error of Nestorius. To all these they added "the letter of the most blessed and holy Archbishop Leo, prelate of the great and ancient city of Rome, written to the Archbishop Flavian, of blessed memory, to correct the perverse interpretation of Eutyches, which letter is in accordance with the confession of the great Peter, and is like a great pillar of truth against erroneous teachers, serving for the confirmation of the true doctrines." They then embody the substance of the letter in their definition, and it is only at the end of this long document, that they use those words, which you have quoted, as referring to the Nicene symbol: "These things, therefore, being arranged by us with all care and diligence, this holy and general synod has defined that it is lawful for no one to utter, write, or compose any other faith, or to think, or to teach others differently."* So far, then, from condemning by anticipation the definitions of Trent, the Council of Chalcedon broadly affirmed the right of the Church at all times to meet the devices of heretics by a more formal and precise definition of the doctrines which are assailed, and added to the ancient symbol a long declaration, which it required all to subscribe, under penalty of forfeiting the communion of the Church. There is no way of jus-

* T. II. Conc. Col. 455.

tifying your restriction of this canon to the Nicene symbol, unless by supposing that you did not read the paragraph in which it occurs. It is for you to explain it. The object of the decree was to prevent any new formulary which might conceal the condemned errors on the points then at issue, and to make it obligatory on all to receive, not only the symbol of Nice in its enlarged form, but also the dogmatical definition of St. Leo. It never entered into the mind of the Council to restrain future councils from exercising the same authority against every novel error.

Your boasting of the Prayer-Book and Catechism is vain, since although written in the vernacular tongue, they give occasion to much discussion as to the true teaching of the Church of England, and her American daughter, and accordingly leave your members uncertain and discordant. We are abundantly provided with means of instruction for all classes, whereby we give them certain knowledge of the doctrines of the Church. They learn the Apostles' Creed from their infancy; they have the Creed of Nice in their Prayer-Book, and use it when assisting at the holy sacrifice, at which it is solemnly sung; and they recite the Athanasian Creed, whenever their devotion prompts them, whilst the clergy are bound to its recital in the office for Sunday. Our Catechisms are plain and explicit. The teaching of the clergy everywhere is uniform, and their efforts to impress the great truths of religion on the minds of their hearers are incessant; so that we have all the advantages which you prize, without the divisions which distract and perplex you. It matters not that each channel of communication be not absolutely free from all danger of error, for from the variety of ways in which we are instructed, publicly and privately, by preaching and in writing, we have full certainty of what the doctrine of the Church is, so that we can give an unqualified assent to her teaching, as she is the pillar and ground of the truth. This necessary foundation of faith is wanting to you. With whatever force the testimonies of Scripture may strike you, however clearly the faith of the ancient church may be expressed in the symbols, however strong may be the language of your Prayer-Book and Catechism, doubt may still haunt your minds, because you have no infallible authority on which to rely. You may persuade yourselves that you have arrived at a correct conclusion, but the Protestant principle of private judgment isolates you, notwithstanding your church connections, and your assent to any revealed doctrine, properly analyzed on your own principles, and by your own showing, amounts to this: I believe that this doctrine is contained in Scripture, because it is in harmony with the primitive interpretation; and I believe such to be the primitive interpretation, because my own judgment convinces me of the fact. This, I respectfully submit, is an act of faith in your own private judgment.

LETTER III.

On the Scripture.

Right Reverend Sir:

DR. MILNER states, that "If Christ had intended that all mankind should learn His religion from a book, namely, the New Testament, he himself would have written that book, and would have laid down as the first and fundamental principle of his religion, the obligation of learning to read it." This you call "an impious attempt to lessen the Divine authority of the Scriptures," "an impious slur upon the Word of God," "an infidel suggestion!" "a most irreverent and blasphemous specimen of argumentation." Abuse is no reply. You should have shown, at least, that Christ supplied the wants of men, by ordering the sacred penmen to write down, either severally, or collectively, His whole revelation; you should have proved that they actually undertook and accomplished the task, and gave the command to all to read the book, with a promise of divine aid to understand it. Instead of this course, you lose patience, because the Catholic apologist points to facts, which show that the inspired books were written on special occasions for particular ends, and do not appear as designed to form a complete collection, or doctrinal summary. Your sixteenth letter is indeed declamatory and abusive, wholly unworthy of a calm disputant. We charge on our Lord no incongruity, since we show that he established a ministry, to deliver all whatsoever He had taught, and He promised to be with them to the end of time. The writing of some books by inspired men did not annul this commission, but facilitated its execution, by recording it, and placing on record likewise, much of that which was to be delivered. All you say about our putting tradition above the written word is mere assertion; we unfeignedly venerate the Scripture, and guard against its abuse by holding fast to the teaching which comes down from the Apostles. The difference between you and us is this, that you affirm that the writing of the books of the New Testament superseded the apostolic commission, inasmuch as the written word was thenceforth to be the sole guide of the teachers in the Church. This we challenge you to prove. We hold that the commission by its very terms extends to the consummation of the world, and that the inspired books must be declared and expounded by the pastors of the Church, in accordance with the faith originally delivered. You say the Apostles were the lawgivers of the Church,—the bishops are judges, who expound the law. We hold that the Apostles were witnesses of what had been revealed, and lawgivers in regard to discipline, and all that appertains to order. They taught not as of themselves, but they merely delivered that which Christ had taught; they being enlightened by the Holy Ghost to deliver it accurately. Their preaching comprised the whole counsel of God. Their writings contained the same things as they preached, but not as fully, or as distinctly as their discourses, incidental references being sometimes made to matters which they had already fully explained by word of mouth. We demand proof that they purposed to give a full written statement of the whole revealed doctrine. They were lawgivers, invested with ample power to legislate for the church; but they have left us no code of laws. Some of their ordinances are found here and there recorded, but nothing like a formal statement of them occurs in the sacred writings. To assign, then, to the bishops of the Church the mere office of judges, confined to the duty of expounding and applying the law, is to circumscribe it within narrow limits. They inherit the governing power granted to the Apostles, and they can consequently make laws for the Church, over which the Holy Ghost has placed them.

You evade, rather than meet the objection of Dr. Milner, that the Church of England has no sufficient evidence of the inspiration of the Bible, by replying: "We have all the evidence that exists, and there can be no more." Not so, dear sir; you must show that you are entitled to use this evidence. There may be an excellent title to an estate, which is not available to any one but the rightful claimant. You accuse Dr. Milner of "an atrocious misrepresentation," as charging the Reformers with rejecting the truth, which the Church of Rome derives from the pure ages of primitive antiquity, because they rejected the errors which she had superadded. This is not the charge. We hold them to be inconsistent in retaining the Bible, whilst they charge with corruption and idolatry the Church, which is its witness and guardian. We challenge you to show why you believe the Bible to be the inspired word of God. Its authenticity, as a collection of books, is not in question. You may prove this as you would that of any profane work: but what certainty have you that it is God's revelation to man? "As for me," says St. Augustin, "I would not believe the Gospel, were I not moved to it by the authority of the Catholic Church."* You reject this authority, and yet you profess to venerate, as divine, all the books which you include in the canon. In separating from the communion of the Catholic Church, the Church of England forfeited all her titles derived from that connection, and in order

* Ep. contra Fundam.

to be a consistent witness to the Bible, she needed a new revelation.

Although many internal indications of its divine origin may be discovered in the Scripture, unqualified faith in its inspiration needs external testimony—no other than the tradition of the Church, which, from the beginning, has been its depositary and guardian. To say that it proves itself, is begging the question. To allege that we know it to be divine by the secret teaching of the Holy Spirit in our hearts, is to open the way to fanatical illusions, and take from it the credibility which might command the respect of unbelievers themselves. The testimony of the Church at present is but the echo of tradition. Dr. Nevin observes: "There is not merely room thus, but an absolute necessity for what may be styled a true Christian *tradition* in the Church, not as something against the Bible or foreign from it; but still not as a mere derivation either, or efflux simply from its pages; a tradition which starts from the original substance of Christianity itself, as it underlies the Bible, and which, in such form, becomes the living stream into which continuously the sense of the Bible is poured, through the Holy Ghost, from age to age, onward to the end of the world."*

Dr. Milner uses the common law of England to illustrate tradition. It comprises all princi-

* Mercersburg Review, July, 1849, Article. The Apostles' Creed.

ples of jurisprudence which have been, from time immemorial, adopted by the judicial tribunals as rules by which the cases submitted to their judgment, and not regulated by special statute, should be decided. The principles themselves do not form a written code, being nowhere recorded, but being gathered from the decisions of the courts. The doctrines handed down by tradition, are in like manner known with certainty from the uniform judgment of the ecclesiastical tribunals. Yet they are far from being destitute of written evidence, since the Scriptures embody most of them, or allude to them; the ancient fathers record them, and the various ecclesiastical documents of the early ages bear witness to them. Besides, they are supported by the public and solemn practices of the Church, in the most ancient times, which are necessarily connected with them. Thus they are recommended to us by evidence far more satisfactory than that which is offered for the common law. You remark that the Church, being a divine institution, could not have mere custom as the origin of her laws. The question is not, indeed, of laws, which certainly might originate in custom, but of revealed doctrines. These could not arise from custom; but public usage, especially in worship, may be one of the evidences of revelation, which is all that Dr. Milner meant by the comparison.

If Christ had given us a written summary of

doctrine, and a code of laws, your reasoning as to the office of bishops as expositors and judges might be just; but as he gave neither, and as the sacred penmen did not profess to give either, the commission to preach remains in its full force, and guarantees the teaching of the Apostolic ministry to the end of time.

You can never determine with certainty the canon of divine books, unless by the testimony and judgment of the Catholic Church. The books which the Church of England treats as apocryphal, were venerated by the whole church as divine during ages. This conviction survived the schism, since even under Edward VI. no distinction was made between the various books, and many passages from them are quoted in the Homilies as dictates of the Holy Ghost. In re-opening the question afterwards, on the plea that they were not included in the Jewish canon, an undue importance was given to it, to the neglect of Apostolic tradition. Even the Hellenist Jews united them in a volume with the inspired writings, as Beveridge testifies,* giving them great authority, and acknowledging them to be highly instructive, although they did not regard them as of the same divine character as the others. From them the early Christians received them with high veneration. S. Augustin observes, "We must not omit those books which were written before the coming of

* Codex Can. Prim. Eccl. l. ii c. ix.

the Saviour, for although they be not received by the Jews, they are received by the church of the Saviour himself."* The doubts which existed for a time in the minds of some fathers regarding their authority, arose from attending to the Jewish canon; but the general tradition of the Church is apparent from their writings, since even they frequently quote the books in question as divine. The canon was settled by the Councils of Carthage and Rome in the fourth and fifth centuries, and by the authority of Popes Innocent and Gelasius. The Council of Florence recognized all the sacred books, precisely as the fathers of Trent afterwards. If some discrepancies be found in certain manuscripts of the ancient catalogues as to the number of the books of the Macchabees, or if some other books be omitted, it belonged to the Church to pronounce judgment on them definitively, and thus settle the matter for ever. Deny her this right, and you leave the Scriptures to be the sport of human pride, one man adding, and another taking away. The words of S. Jerom, that the Church reads them for edification, not with a view to establish dogmas, mean, that she does not rely on their authority for convincing unbelievers; but she has always read them as God's holy word, which all should receive with faith and submission. It is in vain that the Church of England seeks to take shelter under the authority of this father.

* In Speculo.

They who question the right of the Church to put in her canon, books which the Jews did not hold to be inspired, undervalue greatly the tradition of the Apostles. The early Christians read the Scriptures in the Greek version of the Septuagint, which the Apostles always cited, and which contained all the books bound up together. The Apostolic writings and the Gospels have many allusions and references to these books. The earliest fathers, such as Irenæus, quote them like other Scripture. Beveridge testifies, that in the days of St. Cyprian, they were received equally as the other inspired books.* If the doubt which subsisted in the minds of some as to their divine origin should have prevented their acceptance by the Church, how were various books of the New Testament admitted as canonical, although doubts had been entertained of their authority?

The canon of Trent agrees with those of Carthage and of Rome. Baruch was included in the ancient lists under the name of Jeremiah, whose scribe he was. Two books of Macchabees, as in the canon of Carthage, are found in some manuscripts of the council under Gelasius; but if the common reading be retained, it may be that both books were regarded as one, since only one book of Esdras is likewise mentioned. In specifying the parts of Daniel which regard the History of Susanna, and the Hymn of the Three

* Codex Can. Prim. Eccl. l. ii. c. ix.

Youths in the Furnace, you lead the reader to suppose that these were omitted in the ancient lists; whereas, the book of Daniel, as it was read in the churches, included them. The Council of Trent, therefore, only held up to veneration the books which in the fourth and fifth centuries were regarded as canonical. The language of St. Gregory, that the books of the Macchabees do not appertain to the canon, has reference to the Jewish canon. You are wrong in saying that the Church has added to the Bible, "books which the voice of all antiquity had excluded from the canon." The canon of Laodicea, on which you rely, is, in the judgment of some learned critics, supposititious. Paley admits that it had no binding force beyond the province in which it was enacted.*

You have not, Right Reverend Sir, explained how a Church of England-man, or an Episcopalian, can make an act of faith in the divine inspiration of the Scriptures. You call it "folly and effrontery" to doubt of it; "for how can Christian men have faith in anything, if they cannot have it in the written word of God?"† But this is no answer to the question. You say, indeed, that "the law of the Christian faith given to the Church, in the New Testament, could only be identified by the authority of the church:‡ as our general constitution can only

* Evidences of Christianity, ch. ix. § 6. † P. 336. ‡ P. 334.

be known by the testimony of the nation." But if the testimony of the Church be merely human, if it go no farther than to certify the authenticity of the books called the New Testament,—how can you hold them to be the inspired word of God? We recognize the Church by her marks and characters as a divine institution, and we accept her testimony as worthy of all belief, so that we venerate the written word on her authority, as Augustin did. The perusal of it confirms us in our belief of her divine commission. In this proceeding, it is easy to perceive how faith is formed; but you refer to the Church only as to the witness of the written constitution and law of Christ, who gave nothing in writing, and from your examination of what you designate such, you profess to hold her divine constitution. This cannot be faith.

Dr. Milner reproached the Church of England with wilful corruptions of the sacred text. You admit two instances of erroneous translations, but contend that they are of little moment. In return, you charge us with three "grave misrepresentations." Let me first observe that our version cannot be suspected of any design to misrepresent passages applicable to modern controversy, since it was made so many ages before the Reformation. Whether the reading of Genesis iii. 15, be IT or SHE, is a fair matter for critical inquiry, which cannot affect the high character of the Vulgate, which presents a reading received from the days of S. Ambrose.* SACRAMENTUM in Latin corresponds to the Greek Eph. v. 31, and means *mystery*. The English term is not used with a view to ground a controversial argument, but from a close adherence to the Latin, which the Rhemish translator chose to observe. Hooker remarks that the term was used with great latitude by the ancient fathers. The third passage, which you brand as "a very gross perversion" (Hebrew xi. 21), is vindicated by the learned Protestant critic, Tholuck, who says that "the Protestant controversialists have very unjustly designated this passage of the Vulgate, as one of the most palpable of its errors." I need not trouble you with the vindication, which is supported by the authority of S. Chrysostom and Theodoret. Those who choose may find the details in Kitto's Cyclopedia, Art. *Vulgate.* Scrivener is there quoted, who says: "In justice it must be observed, that no case of wilful perversion has ever been brought home to the Vulgate."

You elsewhere charge the Vulgate and Douay versions with not being faithful to the Hebrew, because the term צוּר is rendered in sixteen passages of the Old Testament, "Deus," "God." Had you consulted the Septuagint, you might have included it in the censure, since θέος is the Greek translation. Infidelity on the part of the translator, implies a departure from the meaning of the text, which, however, the ancient inter-

* L. de fuga sæculi, c. vii.

preters have faithfully adhered to, since it is evident that God is figuratively styled a rock. "The God of my salvation," or "God my Saviour," is certainly expressive of the true meaning of all those passages which you render "the Rock of my salvation." Pagnini and Montanus have given the literal sense, which is perfectly consistent with the plainer rendering of the Vulgate. The unlearned reader may be startled at your array of passages, with the Hebrew characters interspersed; but the learned must acknowledge that there is no ground whatever for the charge of unfaithfulness. There is a commandment, "Thou shalt not bear false witness."

You follow on the track of those who rail at the Council of Trent and the Popes, in reference to the authentic edition of the Vulgate. The Council desired a most accurate edition to be made of it, in compliance with which decree, Sixtus V. gave his sanction to one prepared by learned divines, chosen for the purpose. It was soon found to contain about forty typographical errors, which the Pope himself marked for correction. After his death a revision of it was made on a new basis, namely, with special reference to the original texts, which led to several alterations, in a subsequent edition, published with the sanction of Clement VIII. The alleged conflict of authority in respect to these versions, is purely imaginary. The Council sanctioned the Vulgate as a version substantially correct, and a safe standard in faith and morals; but as many discrepancies were found in the readings, the fathers desired that a most accurate version should be prepared. Sixtus V. directed the correctors to confine themselves chiefly to the comparison of manuscripts, so as to give as correctly as possible the true text of the Vulgate. This was successfully done, and the edition was sanctioned by him, which implied no more than that it was to be received and adopted as a standard, which no individual should change. The few typographical errors discovered by him, disposed him to wish for a more accurate edition, which was published by Clement VIII., with many other alterations, to render it more conformable to the original texts. This latter sanction was of the same character, marking the work with the seal of the pontifical approval, so that no private individual might attempt any change in it. Those who prepared it, freely avowed that they left unaltered certain readings which appeared to them capable of improvement. This observation shows the maturity with which they had proceeded, and their slowness to change what further researches might prove to be correct. It also proves that they did not put forward the edition as absolutely perfect, but as substantially correct and safe. You quote the avowal in a tone of triumph, as if it did not do honor to the judgment and candor of the learned men employed in the arduous undertaking. The matter itself—the greater or less accuracy of the edition—did not fall within the range of those things, in which infallibility is claimed by Council or Pontiff. There was no room, therefore, for your exclamation: "There we have, undoubtedly, a fair specimen of your Roman infallibility." There was no occasion to speak of "the audacity" with which Dr. Milner, under such circumstances, could presume to assail the fidelity of "our English Bible."

LETTER IV.

On the Interpretation of Scripture.

Right Reverend Sir:

YOU charge Dr. Milner with proposing tradition as a distinct and additional revelation, independent of the Scriptures, whilst you profess to regard it as the fixed and settled interpretation of the Scriptures in the Church of God. It is of great importance that we should understand each other. Divine tradition, as maintained by the Catholic Church, is not a revelation distinct from the written word, but in its amplest and most correct sense, it includes the Scriptures, since it is the whole revealed doctrine as handed down in the Church from Christ and his Apostles. It certifies the inspiration of the Scriptures; it illustrates them; and it instructs us in several revealed truths, to which they allude or refer, as also in some which are not there recorded. It is properly the entire deposit of doctrine as it comes down from the beginning. This is the idea of it presented by Dr. Milner, whose proofs from S. Irenæus, Tertullian, Origen, Basil, Chrysostom, and Vincent of Lexrins, you seem to have overlooked. I beg to add some few passages. S. Irenæus says: "There being such proofs to look to, we ought not still to seek amongst others for truth which it is easy to receive from the Church, seeing that the Apostles most fully committed unto this Church, as unto a rich repository, all whatsoever is of truth, that every one that willeth may draw out of it the drink of life. For this is the gate of life; but all others are thieves and robbers. Therefore we ought to avoid them, but to cling with the utmost care to whatever is of the Church, and to hold fast to the tradition of truth."* You lay stress on those passages, in which Irenæus refers to the Scriptures; but he expressly qualifies these references by insisting on interpreting them according to the tradition of the Apostles, as manifested in the teaching of the Church by the bishops. He rejects, indeed, the tradition alleged by the Gnostics, who contended that a more perfect doctrine than that which is on record had secretly been communicated by the Apostles to chosen men, and had been preserved in their sect. The Church knows no such clandestine teaching; her tradition has always been publicly taught, and illustrated by her solemn usages, so that it was easily discernible throughout the world for all who sincerely desired in-

* Adv. Hær. l. iii. c. iv.

struction in the truth, as Irenæus observes: "When, on the other hand, we challenge them to that tradition which is from the Apostles, which is preserved in the churches through the successions of presbyters, they are adverse to tradition."*

The early fathers, you allege, appealed to the Scripture as the great means of deciding all controversy. Of Tertullian you say: "He argues all questions of doctrine by appealing to Scripture."† Doubtless, he quoted the Sacred Text whenever he found it opportune and convincing; and he justly rejected the unauthorized teaching of Hermogenes and Marcion, which was void of all Scriptural sanction; but he uniformly rested on the interpretation, which had come down from the Apostles, and which was gathered from the constant teaching of the Church, repudiating in the most unqualified terms all attempts to determine the revealed doctrines by the mere letter of the Scripture, apart from Apostolic tradition. In his work "On Prescriptions," by which he understands barriers against heresy, he advises us not to enter into contests about passages of Scripture, they being easily distorted: "therefore there must be no appeal to the Scriptures, nor must the contest be constituted in those things in which the victory is either none or doubtful, or too little doubtful. For even though the debate of the Scriptures should not so turn

* Ib. c. 2.

† Vol. i. p. 54.

out as to confirm each party, the order of things required that this question should be first proposed, which now is the only one to be discussed, 'To whom belongs the very faith; whose are the Scriptures; by whom, and through whom, and when, and to whom, was that rule delivered whereby men became Christians?' for wherever both the true Christian rule and faith shall be shown to be, there will be the true Scriptures, and the true expositions, and all the true Christian traditions. If these things be so, so that the truth be adjudged to us, as many as walk according to that rule which the Church has handed down from the Apostles, the Apostles from Christ, Christ from God, the reasonableness of our proposition is manifest, which determines that heretics are not to be allowed to enter upon an appeal to the Scriptures, whom we prove without the Scriptures to have no concern with the Scriptures."* From your notice of Tertullian, your readers would scarcely be prepared to find such language from his pen.

Allow me to add another passage from this work: "Now whatt he Apostles preached, that is, what Christ revealed unto them, I will here also rule, must be proved in no other way than by these same churches which the Apostles themselves founded; themselves by preaching to them as well *viva voce*, as men say, as afterwards by epistles. If these things be so, it becomes forth-

* De Præscr, vi. 37.

with manifest that all doctrine which agrees with these apostolic churches, the wombs and originals of the faith, must be accounted true, as without doubt containing that which the churches received from the Apostles, the Apostles from Christ, Christ from God; but that every doctrine must be judged at once to be false, which savoreth things contrary to the truth of the churches, and of the Apostles, and of Christ, and of God. It remains, therefore, that we show whether this our doctrine, the rule of which we have above declared, be derived from the tradition of the Apostles, and from this very fact, whether the other doctrines come of falsehood. We have communion with the apostolic churches, because we have no doctrine differing from them. This is evidence of truth."*

You supply us, Right Reverend Sir, with texts from Clement of Alexandria and other fathers, extolling the Scriptures, as we extol them, but you leave us to present those passages which designate the Church as their necessary interpreter, by means of that apostolic tradition which she preserves. "We children, avoiding the winds of heresies, which puff up to swelling pride, and not believing those who teach otherwise than the fathers, are then perfected, when we are a church having received Christ the head."† Clement defends at large "the celebrated and venerated rule of tradition."‡ Some

* De Praescr, v. 21. † Paedag. l. i. c. v. ‡ Stromat, l. i.

points of a sublimer kind, he says, have been orally transmitted. "Knowledge itself is that which has come down, transmitted without writing to a few by successions from the Apostles." "In the same manner as if one became, from being a man, a brute, as they did who were under the drugs of Circe, so he has ceased to be a man of God, and faithful to the Lord, who has thrown aside the ecclesiastical tradition, and plunged into the opinions of human heresies."*

Origen, you say, "lays down the rule that the ministry must prove everything from Scripture, not according to their private judgment, but by the sense of the Holy Spirit, comparing each passage with the rest."† If by this you understand that he confines the Christian teaching to that which is expressly delivered in the Scripture, you greatly mistake his meaning, for he appeals to apostolic tradition in support of the practice of baptizing infants. The passage on which you rely, occurs in his commentary on St. Matthew, where he speaks of the tradition of the Pharisees opposed to the divine commandment, to honor our parents. Indulging his genius for mystical interpretation, he insists that by an oath, in the text where our Saviour rejects the Pharisaical distinctions of oaths made by the temple and the altar, "must be understood every testimony of Scripture, which is brought

* Ib. l. vii.

† Vol i. p. 65.

forward to confirm and bind fast the word which we utter; so that all Scripture divinely inspired is, indeed, the temple of the glory of God, and its meaning is as gold. We should, therefore, for a testimony of all the words we utter in teaching, bring forward the sense of Scripture; as it were confirming the meaning which we give. For as all gold out of the temple is not sanctified, so every sense which is foreign to the divine Scripture, however admirable it may appear to some, is not holy, because it is not contained in the meaning of the Scripture, which is wont to sanctify that meaning only which it has in itself, as the temple sanctifies its own gold."* From this whole reasoning it is manifest, that Origen is only laboring to show, that we should not attach to the Scripture a meaning foreign to it. He does not say, that the Scripture interprets itself, or that we must not have recourse to the Church to ascertain its meaning in doubtful places. On the contrary, he cautions us against the interpretations of heretics, and against fanciful interpretations of our own, and directs us to adhere to that teaching which is sanctioned by the Church. "We must point out," he says, "the manifest ways to those who hold to the rule of the heavenly Church of Christ, according to the succession from the Apostles."† "Let Basilides and whosoever agrees with him, be

* Vol. xii. p. 35, ed. Wirceburgi.

† T. i. de Princip. p. 164.

left in their impiety; but for us, let us turn to the meaning of the Apostle, according to the piety of the ecclesiastical doctrine."* Again, he observes, "Since there are many who think that their sentiments are conformable to the doctrine of Christ, and some of them think differently from others, let the preaching of the Church, handed down from the Apostles by regular succession, and continuing in the churches down to the present time, be attended to: that only, which in no respect departs from the ecclesiastical and apostolic tradition, is to be believed to be the truth."† These are the views inculcated by this celebrated writer, who, had he himself followed them out in his interpretation of Scripture, would have escaped those errors into which an exuberant imagination betrayed him.

In the defence of the usage of re-baptizing those who had received baptism from heretics, St. Cyprian rejected the proof from tradition, by which the validity of the baptism was defended. You recite his testimony as if you approved his error. If you do not, how do you maintain the contrary by Scripture alone? Cyprian himself strongly insisted on the Lord's tradition for the mingling of water with wine in the chalice.‡

S. Athanasius appealed to the Scriptures as affording splendid proofs of the divinity of our

* l. iv. in Ep. ad Rom. l. v. p. 349.

† De Princ. praef. n. 2.

‡ Ep. lxiii. ad Cornel.

Lord, which was defined in the Council at Nice and declared in the symbol; but he was very far from excluding the tradition of the Church as the light which must guide us in their interpretation: "Let us, nevertheless, in addition to the above, see the tradition which is from the beginning, and the doctrine and faith of the Catholic Church, which the Lord indeed communicated, but the Apostles proclaimed, and the fathers guarded; for on this has the Church been founded, and he who falls away from this, would not be, nor would he ever be called a Christian."* You quote him as saying that the Nicene fathers gave forth the confession of faith, "in order to prove that this was not a new opinion, but Apostolical, and that what they set forth was not their invention, but THE DOCUMENTS OF THE APOSTLES."† The capitals are yours. The text does not say this precisely ταῦτ' ἐστὶν ἅπερ ἐδίδαξαν ὁι ἀποςολοι. The Latin translation gives it literally: "*ea ipsa sunt quæ docuerunt apostoli.*" Your object in giving this turn to the phrase was evidently to limit the teaching of the Apostles to their writings, which the text does not warrant. Is this the fidelity we are to look for in a respectable controvertist?

Nothing can be plainer from all the writings of S. Athanasius, and from the whole proceedings

* Ep. i. ad Serap. n. 28.

† De Syn. Arim. et Seleuciæ Ep. t. i. n. 6. p. 893.

in the case of Arius, than that the Catholic faith was simply propounded as the ancient doctrine, supported by Scripture and tradition. No attempt was made to rest it on Scripture alone; on the contrary, the cavils of the Arians were effectually set aside by referring to the faith as handed down in the Church, which was accordingly put forward as the authoritative expression of divine truth. Do you seriously believe that the mystery of the Incarnation, or the divinity of Jesus Christ, can be sustained by mere Scriptural passages, whilst so many testimonies apparently conflicting are arrayed against them?

The language of S. Cyril of Jerusalem which you recite, is directed to inculcate the mystery of the Incarnation on the authority of the Scriptures, and to recommend the symbol of faith—the creed styled of the Apostles, as a summary of high mysteries taught likewise in the sacred books. No one can mistake it as designed to exclude the traditionary teaching of the Church, on which the creed wholly rests. The necessity of a living authority to expound the creed and the Scriptures appeared most manifestly at that very period, since the fathers of Nice deemed it all-important to add such expressions as would leave no room for the evasions of the Arians.

You might well have spared yourself the recital of the eulogies of S. Jerom on the Scriptures, since in this regard there is no difference between us. You are not very accurate in your translation. S. Jerom relied on the Roman faith, handed down from the days of Peter and Paul, not the mere letter of Scripture—as a protection against the errors of Origen, concerning which Pammachius et Oceanus had consulted him: "Whosoever thou art that assertest new dogmas, I pray thee to spare Roman ears, spare the faith which was praised by the mouth of the Apostle. Why, after four hundred years, dost thou endeavor to teach us what we never knew before? Why dost thou bring forward now what Peter and Paul did not set forth? To this day the Christian world was ignorant of that doctrine?"* Instead of faith which was praised, you have: "*Spare them, because the Romans are praised.*" You put in capitals WHAT PETER AND PAUL WERE UNWILLING TO SET FORTH, leading your readers to imagine that S. Jerom's words are confined to their writing, whereas they plainly embrace their whole teaching as known from the tradition and faith of the Roman Church. In the same spirit he wrote: "Nothing is dearer to us than to guard the rights of Christ, and not to move the landmarks of the fathers, and ever to bear in mind the Roman faith, commended by the mouth of an apostle."†

S. Augustin appealed to the Scriptures as

* Ad Pammach. et Ocean.

† T. I. Ep. lxiii. ad Theoph.

bearing testimony to the Church, especially to her catholic character, but he did not set aside the authority of tradition on points of which they have not distinctly treated. On the contrary, he called the usage of baptizing infants an apostolical tradition;* he maintained "that the dead are aided by the prayers of Holy Church, and by the salutary sacrifice, and by the alms which are offered for their spirits," because "this has been handed down by the fathers;"† and he upheld the validity of baptism administered by heretics on the same principle.‡

This short review of your authorities on this point, proves that the Scriptures were always interpreted in conformity with ecclesiastical tradition, by which means "the faith once delivered to the Saints," was preserved unchanged. When this magnet is not attended to, men necessarily are tossed to and fro by every wind of doctrine. The rule of traditionary interpretation was not limited to any particular period, or any special controversy; it was to serve always and in all circumstances for distinguishing divine truth from human errors.

It has always been the care of the Church to guide her children in the reading of the Scriptures by the light of ancient tradition: for which reason she has caused them to be publicly read

* T. III. de Gen. ad lit. l. x. n. 39.

† T. v. Serm. clxxii. n. 2.

‡ T. ix. l. II. de Bapt. contra Donat. n. 12.

in the celebration of the holy sacrifice, and to be expounded. The private study of them was also strongly recommended by S. Chrysostom, S. Jerom, and other holy fathers; but the scarcity of manuscripts necessarily confined it to few, before the invention of the art of printing. In the thirteenth century, for the first time, some restriction was placed on it, in consequence of its abuse by certain sectaries, who clandestinely assembled, and without authority, took on themselves the office of teachers. Pope Innocent III. avowed that the desire to study the Scriptures, and to draw from them matter of exhortation, is praiseworthy, rather than blamable; yet he rebuked the presumptuous temerity of such sectaries, and forbid the laity to have the books of the Old or New Testament, with the exception of a Psalter, a Breviary, or the Office of the Blessed Virgin. This prohibition grew out of the abuse, and was but local and temporary; yet you do not fail to note it down in order to foment public prejudice. At no time whatever was the Bible a sealed book for the laity, although during the rage of controversy, in the sixteenth century, certain qualifications, namely, instruction and piety, were demanded in the readers. The actual discipline of the Church leaves it entirely free, provided the version be approved, and have notes taken from Catholic sources.* You

* See Addition to IV. Rule of Index Decr. S. Cong. Ind., 13 Junii, 1757.

assert that "the Church has forbidden the laity to have the Bible in the vulgar tongue, by the decrees of many Popes and Councils, and has only allowed it since the Reformation, under great restrictions, through fear and necessity." The contrary is the fact. No such general prohibition was ever made. The Fourth Rule of the Index, which imposes the simple restrictions above stated, was a consequence of the abuses which marked the Reformation, and even these restrictions have been removed in regard to all approved versions. Pius VI., in accepting the Italian translation of the Bible by Martini, Archbishop of Florence, expressly said that the Scriptures should be left open to all, to draw from them purity of morals and of doctrine, and to eradicate the most corrupt errors which are prevalent. It is a singular fact, yet incontrovertible, that the first restrictions on the reading of the Bible in English, emanated from Henry VIII. by Act of Parliament.* "The Holy Bible," as Sir Thomas More attests, "was long before Wickliffe's days, by virtuous and well learned men translated into the English tongue, and by good and godly people, with devotion and soberness, well and reverently red."†

* 34th Henry VIII. 1. † Dial. iii. 14.

LETTER V.

On the Sacraments.

Right Reverend Sir:

AS Dr. Milner and yourself are not greatly at variance in regard to the definition of a sacrament, I shall not enter into any discussion on the subject. In the Catholic view some outward or sensible sign is required, to which grace is attached by the institution of Christ. You deny that confirmation can be considered such, because its divine institution is not recorded, and there is no visible sign or symbol of the grace conferred. We deem this an instance fit to illustrate the doctrine of tradition. From the fact, which is stated by the sacred historian, that Peter and John, at the instance of the other Apostles, went to Samaria, to impart the Holy Ghost to the neophytes whom Philip had baptized, and that by prayer and the imposition of hands, the Holy Ghost was, in effect, communicated, we infer the divine institution of this rite, since the acts of the Apostles furnish the best evidence of the power given to them by Christ. This inference is supported by the perpetual usage of the Church, which has always recognized in her prelates the same power. Tradition, then, supports our reasoning on the Scripture, and illustrates what is compendiously stated by the sacred penman. There is a visible sign, namely, the laying on of hands with prayer, for although this action might be indefinite in itself, it is determined, by the accompanying prayer, to mark the descent of the Holy Spirit on the candidates. It is not necessary to determine the precise time of the institution, it being sufficient to know that the Apostles must have had a divine warrant to undertake it. Our theologians conjecture, with great probability, that during the forty days after the resurrection, in which our Lord appeared to His disciples, "speaking of the kingdom of God,"* He instructed them on this and other points, for, as St. Leo well remarks, "these forty days, between the resurrection and ascension, did not pass away idly, but great sacraments were confirmed in them, great mysteries were revealed."† The anointing with chrism in performing this rite is a very ancient usage, of which mention is made by Tertullian, in the second century. This warrants the presumption that it was practised and prescribed by the Apostles; nor is the silence of the historian any proof to the contrary, since it is clear that he took on him to state facts, without entering into details of rites or ceremonies. Granting that it is only of

* Acts i. 3.

† Serm. 1, de Ascensione, n. 2.

ecclesiastical origin, it is still venerable for its antiquity, and is an apt symbol to express the unction of the Holy Spirit. You mistake in supposing that we substitute it for the laying on of hands;* since the extension of the hands of bishops over all who await confirmation, accompanied by a solemn prayer to God to send down His Holy Spirit, with His sevenfold gifts, is itself a laying on of hands.

Penance does not appear to you entitled to be regarded as a sacrament. Inasmuch as the Scriptures always commanded repentance, you argue that it could not have been instituted by Christ. Could He not give to the act of the penitent a sacramental virtue, by attaching to it pardon, to be pronounced by His representative? What He actually vouchsafed to do is inscribed on the sacred pages. He gave to His Apostles the power of remitting and retaining sin, in which is necessarily included the right to take cognizance of the sins to be remitted or retained. You say that auricular confession and sacerdotal absolution were the work of the thirteenth century. Yet you had before you the testimonies of Tertullian, Origen, Basil, Paulinus, and Augustin, quoted by Dr. Milner, which clearly prove that confession of sin was made to the priests in their respective times, even as far back as the second century. St. Pacianus and St. Ambrose

* P. 307.

speak of absolution granted to penitents, by the commandment of Christ our Lord.

Extreme unction, although plainly commanded by St. James, the Apostle, is expunged by Protestants from the roll of the sacraments. You maintain that the text has reference to a miraculous operation, by which sick persons recovered health. Is it probable that a regular mode for effecting miraculous cures was prescribed by the Apostle? Were miracles directed to be wrought by a certain class—the presbyters? Was a cure to be effected in all cases, so as to become an ordinary occurrence? Such is not the view which the Scriptures give us of the wonders of Divine power, which are wrought in extraordinary cases to attest revealed truth, or show forth the Divine attributes. The promise of our Lord, that His disciples should lay hands on the sick, and effect their cure, cannot be understood of a uniform or frequent act, but of occasional displays of the power and goodness of God, through the agency of His ministers and servants. You cannot explain the anointing as a laying on of hands, since you deny it to be such in the rite of confirmation. The prayer of faith, to which the salutary effect of the act is ascribed, is justly understood of the words which are uttered whilst the sick man is anointed. The Greek term σώσει, rendered "will save," in scriptural usage, means to sanctify, or to secure the eternal salvation of the soul. The term, ἐγείρει, "raise him up," may be explained of exciting, or animating, as well as of restoring to health, and it is verified by the communication of grace, whereby the sick person is supported in his last agony. You observe "that not the anointing, but the prayer of faith, shall save the sick, and the Lord shall raise him up." The mere anointing could have no virtue, unless its sacramental character were determined by the accompanying prayer, as St. Augustin observes in regard to baptism: "Take away the word, and what is water but water? The word is added to the element, and the sacrament is completed."* A few lines above, you referred the effect to the laying on of hands, according to the prediction of our Saviour, and now you maintain that it results wholly from the prayer. The sickness of which the Apostle speaks is, that which is attended with danger of death, the Greek term ἀσθενεῖ, being the same as is employed when Lazarus was reported to be in a dying state.† The effects of the sacraments arising from their Divine institution, are properly ascribed to God, who alone can pardon sin, and confer the gifts of grace; the priest being only His agent, and the representative of Christ. Thus, sir, all your objections are shown to be groundless, whilst this rite, which has always been practised in the Church, is warranted by

* Tract lxxx. in Joan. † John x. 3.

the express words of Holy Writ. Tradition here serves to illustrate and enforce this apostolic precept, which, strangely enough, is wholly neglected by sects professing aloud that they are guided in all things by the written word. It ill becomes you to designate the faithful observance of the apostolic command "a pious fraud." It is, at least, very unprofitable, since nothing whatever is received on occasion of its performance.

You deny the sacramental character of orders, because they are confined to one small class of men. Are they not of sufficient importance to have grace attached to them for their proper exercise? You admit that they were instituted by Christ; but you remark that priests and Levites were already of long standing, divinely instituted. Was it not worthy of Christ to bestow on His ministers greater gifts, as well as higher powers? You say, that the Apostles, in ordination, used only the imposition of hands, with prayer. If to this simple rite was attached the communication of power for the office, with grace to enable them to exercise it, it is sufficient to give it the character of a sacrament. But it is wrong to infer that the rite was absolutely so simple, from the terms used by the sacred historian, since it was foreign to his purpose to enter into liturgical details. It was, indeed, when sacrificing, or performing solemn worship, that the command was given by the Holy Ghost, to set apart Paul and Barnabas, for the special work intrusted to them, as was accordingly done by the laying on of hands and by prayer. Although we are not informed that other ceremonies were used, there is nothing in this brief statement that necessarily excludes them. Of the grace bestowed we have the testimony of St. Paul, who admonishes Timothy to stir up the grace which was given him by the laying on of hands.*

You find still greater objections to regarding marriage as a sacrament, since it was instituted in Paradise. Yet, even then it was a mysterious type of the future union of Christ with His Church, as the Apostle assures us. It was worthy of our Lord to give it sacramental dignity and character, when that union was consummated by His incarnation. The reasoning of the Apostle on it shows its holiness and sublime signification. The indissoluble force of the marriage tie, which our Lord Himself declares, persuades us that grace must be given to enable the parties to bear the perpetual yoke. His presence at the wedding of Cana, and the miracles which He there performed, show His sanction and favor. So many scriptural indications are supported by the public and solemn teaching of the Church, her perpetual usage and tradition. Although none are obliged to marry, it is consoling to those who choose this state of

* 2 Tim. i. 6.

life, to know that it is not only lawful, but attended with grace and Divine blessing for such as properly enter into it. The Church is perfectly consistent in teaching, with St. Paul, that the state of celibacy is preferable, which leaves the soul at liberty to devote herself wholly to the things of God, and yet assuring her children that they do not sin by embracing the married state, if they take care to prepare themselves for the grace which is attached to the sacred contract.

St. Augustin, in the passage which you quote, speaks of the small number of the Christian sacraments compared with the Jewish rites, which were called by the fathers in the same way. He gives baptism and the communion as instances, without meaning to confine the term to them. The like occurs in his first discourse on the ciii. Psalm, where speaking of the gifts of God bestowed alike on the good and wicked, he observes that even the sacraments are received by them. "Look to the gifts of the Church herself. The gift of the sacraments in baptism, in the Eucharist, in the other holy sacraments, how great a gift it is! Even Simon the magician obtained it." In another place he describes the eagerness of the dying to receive the aids of religion, in these terms: "Do we not reflect that, when the extreme danger is at hand, and there is no possibility of escape, great is the rush of persons, of both sexes and of every age, in the Church, some demanding baptism, others reconciliation, others the assigning of penance itself, all of them seeking consolation, and the celebration and dispensation of the sacraments?"*

You make us, Right Reverend Sir, great reproaches in regard to the exactions practised in the administration of the sacraments, of which you allege some instances within your own knowledge. You assure us that some Canadians applied to you to have their children baptized, being unable to pay the fees demanded by the priest. I cannot suppose that they were residents of Canada, for the discipline of that country rigorously forbids the acceptance of the smallest fee or offering on such an occasion, and the high reputation of the clergy warrants me in believing that it is most strictly observed. Besides, the journey from the nearest part of Canada to Burlington, would cost far more than the most avaricious priest could demand. I must, then, believe that the application came from Canadians, who had settled in your town, and I must refer you for explanation to your old neighbor and correspondent, who will no doubt satisfy you that you have been imposed upon. It is seldom that any even nominal Catholics can be induced in any circumstances to avail themselves of Protestant ministrations.

"Quodcumque ostendis mihi sic, incredulus odi."

* Ep. clxxx. ad Honoratum.

LETTER VI.

Transubstantiation.

RIGHT REVEREND SIR:

JEREMY TAYLOR volunteered his vindication of Catholics from the charge of idolatry in adoring the Eucharist, because our intention is directed to Jesus Christ, our Lord, whom we believe to be present.* Dr. Milner claimed our acquittal on the same ground; but you, kindly as you profess to be disposed, reject the plea, and insist that compared with the Pantheism of the old Egyptians, the incarnation of the Grand Llama, the adoration of the sun by the Aztecs, and the whole range of heathenism, transubstantiation is the "most inconsistent kind of idolatry, and the most degrading to a proper conception of the Deity." Yet you might have paused before uttering these censures, since we have, at least, the respectable authority of St. Augustin for adoring this mystery. Commenting on the passage, "adore His footstool," which the Protestant version renders "worship at His footstool," he says, "Since He (Christ) walked in the flesh, and He has given us the same flesh to

* Liberty of Prophesying, sect. xx.

eat for our salvation, and no one eats without first adoring it, we find how this footstool of the Lord may be adored, so that not merely are we free from sin in adoring it, but we sin, if we do not adore it."*

Your Catechism states, that the inward part of the sacrament is the Body and Blood of Christ, which "are spiritually taken and received by the faithful in the Lord's Supper;" and yet you do not believe them to be really there, since it is only by an effort of faith that you become partakers of them. You insist that "the divine gift *is* in the sacrament, considered with respect to its inward grace."† Your whole reasoning shows, however, that you do not hold the Body and Blood to be really there, so that you can only mean that the sacrament is directed to awaken faith, by which you may receive their virtue; but how can the faithful, as Dr. Milner asks, take that which is not there? Hence it is that so many of the Puseyites, and others, profess to believe in the real presence, which you very evidently reject.

For the variations of your liturgy in this respect, you plead that it was only by degrees that the eyes of the English Reformers were opened. Let this plea have its full force.

In canvassing our evidence, you at once meet

* Enarr. in Ps. xcviii.

† Vol. ii. p. 138.

the proofs from the sixth chapter of St. John by a long commentary of St. Augustin, who, like the other fathers, often indulges in moral applications, or mystical interpretations of the sacred text. The carnal understanding of the words of our Redeemer is justly rejected. "Do you think that I am about to divide this Body, which you behold, into parts, and cut my members into pieces, and give them to you?" He insists on our eating spiritually, that is, receiving the sacrament with such dispositions as will make it profitable to our souls. "Then the Body and Blood of Christ will be life to every one of you, if that which is visibly taken in the Sacrament be spiritually eaten and spiritually drank in the truth itself. For we have heard the Lord Himself saying, 'It is the spirit that quickeneth; the flesh profiteth nothing. The words which I have spoken unto you are spirit and life.'"* If any doubt could exist as to the spiritual eating and drinking here spoken of, it must vanish when we attend to these other words of the same father. "With faithful heart and mouth we receive the Mediator of God and men, the man Christ Jesus, giving us His Flesh to eat, and His Blood to drink, although it seems more shocking to eat human flesh, than to destroy it, and to drink human blood, than to shed it."† In giving rules for the right

* Apud Hopkins, vol. ii. p. 141.

† L. ii. contra advers. legis et proph.

understanding of Scripture, he observes, that in case the Scripture appear to enjoin anything criminal or cruel, it must be regarded as a figure of speech, and he applies this rule to the saying of our Lord, "Unless you eat the flesh of the Son of man, and drink His Blood, you shall not have life in you." This taken as it sounds seems to enjoin a crime, or outrage, namely cannibalism. "It is, therefore, a figure, which intimates that we should commune with the passion of the Lord, and sweetly and profitably treasure up in memory, that his flesh was crucified and bruised for us."* The manifest scope of this passage is to remove the idea of eating the flesh, and drinking the blood of Christ, in a natural and carnal way. Augustin justly insists that this cannot be the meaning, because it implies what is unnatural and revolting. It must then, he says, be understood of communing with the passion of our Lord, remembering his sufferings, and thus becoming partakers of his merits. This explanation is not directed to exclude the sacramental perception of his body and blood, which in the place above quoted St. Augustin distinctly affirms. The language is strictly applicable to sacramental communion, since whilst we receive His Body and Blood under the veils of the elements, we should commemorate his passion and death, according to his command.

* De doct. Christ. l. iii. c. xvi.

You adduce Augustin again, to destroy the force of the words of the institution. He teaches that the sacraments having a certain resemblance to the things which they are intended to represent, take the names of the things themselves. "Therefore, according to a certain mode, the sacrament of Christ's Body is the Body of Christ, and the sacrament of Christ's Blood is the Blood of Christ; and in like manner the sacrament of Faith is Faith."* This language is intended to convey to us that what strikes the senses in this sacrament—the visible species—is styled the Body of Christ, because it is such after a certain mode, inasmuch as it marks the presence of His Body. In speaking of so great a mystery, it was difficult to use words not liable to be misunderstood. Whatever obscurity may arise from occasional expressions of this kind, is dissipated by the clear and positive terms which are elsewhere employed. Thus, speaking of the converted Jews, he says: "Through grace they drank the very blood which they shed in frenzy."†

The last passage which you object from the same father, admits of a similar solution: "Our Lord did not hesitate to say, 'This is My Body,' when he gave them the sign of His Body."‡ Bread, which had been of old a sign, or type, became the Body of Christ, being changed into it by his word, when he instituted this sacrament.

* Op. Aug. t. ii. p. 203, n. 9. † In Ps. lxv. n. 5.
‡ Contra Adimantum, c. xii.

Speaking of it elsewhere, he says: "We are fed with the cross of the Lord, since we eat his Body."*

Persons unacquainted with the style of Tertullian, who refers often to a remote antecedent, may easily mistake the words which you quote: "Our Lord, taking the bread and distributing it to His disciples, made it His Body, by saying: THIS IS MY BODY; that is, the figure of my body."† His meaning is, that what had been the figure of his body, was made his body. He interpreted a passage of Jeremiah, wherein mention was made of bread, as a type of the body of Christ, and showed against Marcion, that Christ recognized the works of the Creator, since he used bread for the holiest purpose, changing it into His Body in the mysteries. When speaking directly and expressly of the Eucharist, his language is most unequivocal: "The flesh," he says, "feeds on the Body and Blood of Christ, that the soul may be fattened of God."‡ Of the returning Prodigal he says: "He is fed with the richness of our Lord's Body, that is, with the Eucharist."§ Speaking of Christian statuaries, who made idols for sale, and afterwards approached the holy table, as if guiltless, because they had not joined in their worship, he says: "They lay their hands on the Body of the Lord." Of those who advanced to the priesthood, with-

* In Ps. c. n. 9.
† Adv. Marcion, l. iv. 457.
‡ L. de resur. carn.
§ De Pudicitia, 9.

out having expiated the sin, he exclaims: "O! enormity! the Jews offered violence to Christ but once; these men violate His Body daily. O! hands that should be cut off!"*

You dispose rather summarily of the text of the martyr Ignatius, quoted by Dr. Milner. Speaking of certain heretics of that early period, he says: "They do not admit of Eucharists and oblations, because they do not believe the Eucharist to be the flesh of our Saviour Jesus Christ, that which suffered for our sins."† You observe, that it is not stated whether Ignatius meant the flesh of our Saviour, in actual substance, or in symbol, or figure. The natural import of the words leaves no room for doubt. What say you to Justin? "As Jesus Christ, our Saviour, was made flesh through the word of God, and took flesh and blood for our salvation, so we have been instructed that the food which has been consecrated by His word of prayer . . . . . is the flesh and blood of that Incarnate Jesus."‡

It is not necessary to dwell on the passages which you have adduced from Origen and Ambrose, in order to destroy the force of the testimonies brought forward by Dr. Milner. The intelligent reader, having in view the remarks already made, will easily distinguish between expressions regarding a mystery incidentally mentioned, and the plain and positive declara-

* L. de idololatria. † Vol. ii. p. 148. ‡ Apol. i. 66.

tion of its nature solemnly delivered: "This Body which we consecrate," says St. Ambrose, "is from the Virgin."* "You may, perhaps, say that which I see is something different; how do you prove to me that I receive the Body of Christ? This is what it remains for me to prove. What examples, therefore, am I to use? Let me prove that this is not that which nature has made it, but that which the benediction hath consecrated it to be; and that the force of the benediction is greater than that of nature, because by the benediction nature herself is changed."† "Our Lord Jesus Christ Himself proclaims, *This is My Body.* Before the sacred words of benediction another species is named; after consecration the Body is implied. He Himself speaks of His Blood. Before consecration, it is spoken of as another thing: after consecration, it is named Blood. And you say, Amen, that is, it is true. What your mouth expresses, let your inner mind confess—feel what you say."‡

It will be difficult to persuade any impartial reader of St. Cyril of Jerusalem, that his very emphatic language concerning the Eucharist loses all its meaning, because he employs occasionally comparisons which are not in all respects adequate. He asks most solemnly: "Since, then, Christ Himself declares and says of the bread, 'This is My Body,' who will dare hence-

* L. de his qui mysteriis initiantur, c. ix.

† De Mysteriis, ix. 50. ‡ Ib. 54.

forward doubt? and since he affirms and says, 'This is My Blood,' who shall ever doubt, and say that it is not His blood? At Cana, of Galilee, he once changed water into wine, which resembles blood, and shall we think him unworthy of belief, when He changes wine into blood?"* The term ἀντίτυπον, used by him, as also in the liturgies, properly denotes that which corresponds to the type, the reality of which the type was the shadow. It is used, however, for the sacramental species, or sensible elements, by St. Cyril, who nevertheless expresses the mystery in the most unequivocal way: "Do not look to them as mere bread and wine, for they are the Body and Blood of Christ, according to the affirmation of our Lord."†

The second Council of Nice justly rejected the language of the Iconoclasts, who called the Eucharist the image of his vivifying Body, although even these did not mean to deny the real presence. As the term was equivocal, it was prudently set aside. Their reasoning on it is conclusive in the circumstances, although it cannot determine the force of some terms used by ancient writers, whose meaning is to be gathered from the context. It is unnecessary to explain the passages objected from St. Isidore, who wrote in the same spirit of faith. The disputes

* Cat. xxii.

† Ibidem. See La Perpétuité de la Foi, vol. iv. l. i. ch. iv. Also Wilberforce on the Eucharist, ch. viii. s. 1.

between Paschasius and his adversaries regarded rather the language than the substance of the mystery. Berenger, in the eleventh century, was the first who boldly questioned the doctrine. His errors, which excited general opposition, were abjured by himself, by order of various councils and popes. There is reason to hope that he died in the communion of the Church.

Because St. Cyprian explains the mystic signification of the mixing of water with wine in the chalice, the water serving to represent the people, the wine representing the Blood of Christ, and explains the grains of wheat, of which the bread is formed, as signifying the union of all the faithful, you conclude that he must have been a stranger to the doctrine of Transubstantiation. If you examine the passages more attentively, you will easily discover your mistake. He insists on the mingling of water with wine, in conformity with the tradition which had come down from the Apostles, certifying that our Lord had tempered the sacramental wine with water; and he took occasion to show, that as waters in the Scripture sometimes represent the people, and wine is employed in the mystery of Christ's Blood, the union was full of signification. In like manner he dwelt on the perfect union of the members of Christ, of which the grains of wheat, formed into bread for sacramental uses, are apt symbols. All this is instructive, but does not regard the nature of the sacrament itself. When Cyprian speaks of apostates who approach communion, without having performed suitable penance, in order to manifest his horror for their crime, he says: "they seize on the Body of the Lord,"—"violence is offered by them to His Body and Blood."* Whoever will read the entire work "On the Fallen," will be satisfied that he not only believed the real presence of the Body and Blood of Christ in the sacrament, but bore testimony to several miracles, by which unworthy communicants were divinely punished.

The language of St. Jerom, which you object, admits the like explanations. He spoke of wine as having been a type of the Blood of Christ, and as being a suitable element to be employed in the mysteries. He considered Melchisedech, in his offering of bread and wine, as foreshadowing the reality of the Body and Blood of Christ, to be presented in the new dispensation. He said that our Lord transfigured His Body into bread, taking its appearance, as it was an apt symbol of the Church, and forming His Blood in the cup, mixed with wine and water, which were changed into it by His power. When he is speaking professedly of the sacrament, he uses language that leaves no room for doubt. "WE ALL ALIKE RECEIVE THE BODY OF CHRIST."† Again, speaking of bishops, he writes: "God

* L. de lapsis.

† L. ii. contra Iovinian.

forbid that I should say anything disrespectful of those who succeed to the rank of the Apostles, and consecrate the Body of Christ with their own mouth."* He says, "that deacons ought not to rank with priests, by whose prayers the Body and Blood of Christ are consecrated."†

You ask, Right Reverend Sir, "How does the literal meaning of our Lord's words: 'This is My Blood, which is shed for you,' agree with the unquestionable fact that His blood was not actually shed for them until the following evening?" By recalling to your recollection the Hebrew manner of using the tenses, you will easily understand that what was soon to take place, is expressed by the present participle: the evangelists having retained their Hebrew style in writing in Greek. Hence the old Latin interpreter translates it in the future. It may also be understood, with great propriety and strictness, of the mystical immolation then made under the sacramental veils, our Lord anticipating the bloody offering of the cross, by presenting Himself as victim in the sacrifice which He instituted. Bishop Wilson takes it in this sense, which is also literal: "He then, at that instant, gave His Body and Blood a sacrifice for the sins of the world."‡ The figure by which the vessel is taken for its contents is so familiar that every one understands it, without any special notice

* Ep. i. ad Heliodorum. † Ep. ci. ad Evangel.

‡ Holy Bible, *with Notes*, quoted in Tract No. 81.

being given. It does not warrant the supposition that the whole sentence is figurative. The different terms used by the sacred writers in recording it, explain one another. The breaking of bread for distribution was equivalent to the giving of it, and as our Lord gave His Body to the Apostles under the appearance of bread, and broke and gave the sacramental elements, both terms are used by the inspired writers, not figuratively but literally. As Archdeacon Wilberforce justly observes: "It is difficult to understand how the Holy Eucharist can depend upon the principle of representations, because why should bread and wine represent our Lord's Body and Blood, except there were some real connection between them? The elements have no natural likeness to flesh and blood, nor, unless the sacramental principle be admitted, have they any special fitness to represent such objects."* Your great array of scriptural passages in which the verb substantive is equivalent to signify, or represent, was unnecessary, because all must admit that in parables, similitudes, allegories, or other like forms of speech, where resemblance or representation is avowedly treated of, the verb substantive has such force, being a convenient and short way of expression, which in the circumstances implies no ambiguity. This, however, does not warrant us in giving it such a meaning, when a solemn covenant is in ques-

* Wilberforce, on the Eucharist, ch. v.

tion. Our Lord was not then engaged in proposing a parable. He was instituting, as we believe, a sacrament and sacrifice. He was near the consummation of His earthly career. He addressed His confidential friends, His disciples, to whom He was wont to speak plainly. He was doing an act which was to continue to be performed in His name to the end of time. It was most important that its nature should be well understood. In these circumstances He was likely to speak plainly and distinctly. Foreknowing that His words would be taken by the vast majority of His followers in their literal and obvious meaning, He surely would have taken care to prevent an error, which, according to you, has resulted in the most degrading idolatry. Four inspired writers have recorded His words, without any variation, as regards those used in consecrating the bread: "This is My Body." Being the only instance, as one of the Tract writers remarks, in which the words of our Lord are recorded exactly the same by four inspired writers, it implies that they are in a high degree mysterious.

We do not set aside the testimony of the senses as to all natural objects, for which they were given us by our Creator, when we hold that God requires us to form our judgment of a revealed mystery on His testimony declared by His Church, without regard to the impressions made on them. Divine mysteries rest solely on

His revelation. Miracles wrought in confirmation of revealed truth fall under the senses; but the sacramental change is not a miracle in this sense. It is, indeed, a secret operation of Divine Power, directed to convey to men a heavenly gift, and to present to God the victim of Calvary.

In regard to the apparitions to the patriarchs you observe: "Their senses were not misled. They saw what was presented to their eyes, correctly. They heard what was presented to their ears correctly. There was no error in *the senses.* But whether the being who addressed them was the Deity, or an angel, or a man, *was not a question for the senses to determine.*"* Was then a real body present? If impressions were made on the senses, without a real object before them, such as the senses reported, then were the patriarchs deceived, until from some other source they learned their error. In the Eucharist the species remain, and make corresponding impressions on the senses; whether the substance be there, or no, *is not a question for the senses to determine.* They only report impressions, which ordinarily warrant the judgment that the natural substance is present. In case of a divine act by which the substance is changed without a change of the appearances, the senses are not at fault, but the observer is mistaken in his judgment, which should not be formed from the impressions, but should rest

* Vol. ii. p. 177.

on the word of God. Your observation, then, is applicable to the Eucharist; for if the patriarchs seeing, hearing, touching their guests, were deceived in regarding them as men, it is evident that in supernatural and mysterious works the senses must not be wholly and absolutely relied on. Hence St. Cyril of Jerusalem thus addressed the faithful: "Contemplate therefore the bread and wine not as bare elements, for they are, according to the Lord's declaration, the Body and Blood of Christ; for though sense suggest this to thee, let faith stablish thee. Judge not the matter from taste, but from faith be fully assured, without misgiving, that thou hast been vouchsafed the Body and Blood of Christ." "Be fully persuaded, that what seems bread is not bread, though bread by taste, but the Body of Christ; and that what seems wine is not wine, though the taste will have it so, but the Blood of Christ."*

You insist that Dr. Milner forces Hooker and other divines of the English Church to bear testimony to the real presence against their will. It is certain that most of your divines qualify their admissions of truth so as to destroy them, or contradict themselves. You know, however, that the Tractarians collected many passages, which they considered fragments of the Catholic doctrines which remained here and there in the

* Oxford Transl. p. 272.

writings of former divines of the Establishment, especially in regard to the Eucharist. Bishop Andrews replied to Bellarmine: "Christ said: 'This is my Body;' in this, the object, we are agreed with you, the manner only is controverted. We hold by a firm belief that it is the Body of Christ." "It is inquired," says Bishop Taylor, "whether when we say we believe Christ's Body to be *really* in the sacrament, we mean *that Body, that Flesh that was born of the Virgin Mary*, that was crucified, dead, and buried. I answer that I know none else that he had or hath; there is but one Body of Christ, natural and glorified; but he that says that Body is glorified which was crucified, says it is the same Body, but not after the same manner, and so it is in the sacrament, we eat and drink the Body and Blood of Christ, that was broken and poured forth; for there is no other Body, no other Blood of Christ; but though it is the same which we eat and drink, yet it is in another manner."* Dr. Pusey, you recollect, startled many by his bold assertion of the Real Presence, and Archdeacon Wilberforce, whilst still in the communion of the English Church, maintained Transubstantiation. Archdeacon Dennison is now arraigned for the same obnoxious tenet, or something approaching it. Yet I freely grant that most of your writers who have spoken in this way, have had little conception of our doc-

* The Real Presence of Christ, sec. i. ii.

trine, and have vacillated in its belief, if not manifestly involved themselves in contradiction. It is a mystery which few can grasp firmly, even in the apprehension of the mind, unless those whom God vouchsafes to draw within His Church. Others occasionally feel the force of the words of Christ, and profess their belief in a Real Presence; but how it is they know not, and seldom care to inquire. The reason is that which S. Augustin assigned for the vague replies of a catechumen when questioned as to this mystery itself: "Jesus has not intrusted Himself to him."*

* Tract. xi. in Joan.

LETTER VII.

On the Sacrifice.

Right Reverend Sir:

YOU very unnecessarily brand Dr. Milner's definition of sacrifice as Deistical, because it includes no mention of Christ. From the statement of St. Paul, that Abel by faith offered to God a more acceptable sacrifice than that of Cain, you infer that his reference of the victim to a future Redeemer constituted the chief value of his offering. It is not quite clear to me that the term *faith* as there employed, imports this distinct recognition. But, at all events, this regards the disposition which rendered the sacrifice more acceptable, and does not properly enter into the definition. Your attempt to extend the term to acts of praise, prayer, compunction, beneficence, is apparently justified by many scriptural texts, which, however, do not treat of sacrifice strictly so called. The prophecy of Malachi has indeed reference to true sacrifice, although the text means rather the offering of incense, an accompaniment of sacrifice, and an oblation of a minor class, such as flour and oil with incense. You confidently appeal to the fathers for its right interpretation, and I cheerfully accept the proposition, being willing to abide by their testimony when they profess to give the literal and strict exposition of the passage.

You begin with Tertullian. Allow me to go still farther back, to St. Justin, the Martyr, who in his dialogue with Tryphon, a Jew, thus descants on the text in question: "Malachi, even at that time speaking of the sacrifices of us gentiles, which are offered in every place, that is, the bread of the Eucharist, and in like manner the wine of the Eucharist, foretold that we indeed should glorify His name, which you profane." He does not here unfold the mystery, but he fixes the literal sense of the prophecy, as regarding the Eucharistic oblation. St. Irenæus gives the like explanation. "Christ took in his hands the bread, which is created, and gave thanks saying: 'This is My Body.' And in like manner He avowed to be His Blood the chalice, which is of that created substance which is with us, and He taught a new offering of the New Covenant, which the Church receiving from the Apostles, offers to God throughout the whole world, to Him who gives us nourishment, the first fruits of His gifts in the New Testament, of which Malachi, one of the twelve prophets, thus foretold." He then recites the entire passage, and adds: "By these words he more manifestly intimates that the ancient people indeed ceased to offer to God, and that in every place sacrifice is offered to God, and this a pure one, and His name is glorified among the nations."* This ancient father distinctly explains the prophecy of the Eucharistic sacrifice.

With these two interpreters of highest antiquity on my side, I can afford to give you the benefit of the exposition of Tertullian, who understands contrition, praise, prayer, to be the sacrifices everywhere offered. Yet it would be unjust to him to suppose, that in presenting these views to Jews, or to a wild sectary, like Marcion, he necessarily excluded the obvious interpretation given by those fathers who preceded him. He elsewhere says: "We sacrifice for the welfare of the Emperor."†

St. Augustin adheres to the literal exposition, and connects it with the celebrated passages of Genesis and the Psalms, regarding the priesthood of Melchisedech: "Since they see that this sacrifice is offered everywhere from the rising to the setting of the sun, by priests according to the order of Melchisedech, they can no longer deny that the sacrifices of the Jews, of whom it is said: 'I have no pleasure in you,' have ceased."‡ This unequivocal language gives us the key to those passages in which he treats of

* L. iv. de hær. c. xxxii. † L. ad Scapulam, c. ii.

‡ L. xviii. de civ. Dei. c. xxxv.

spiritual offerings, acts of self-denial, and of consecration to God. The edifying address to the new communicants, which you have given to your readers, was intended to excite them to offer themselves in sacrifice, by the exercises of a holy life, and on that account he insists on their becoming what they had received, by offering themselves victims to the Divine glory. There is nothing in it which does not harmonize with the mystery. In the same spirit is to be understood his definition of sacrifice in his book on the City of God. When he says, elsewhere, that in "the oblation and participation of the Body and Blood of Christ, Christians celebrate the memorial of His finished sacrifice,"* he speaks of the sacrifice of the altar, which is at once the memorial and application of that complete atonement offered on the cross. Speaking of the Jews, he says: "The passover, which they still celebrate by the offering of a sheep, is different from ours, which we take in the Body and Blood of the Lord."†

Mede, quoted by the Tractarians, remarks on the prophecy of Malachi: "This place of Scripture, however now in a manner silenced and forgotten, was once, and that in the oldest and purest time of the Church, a text of eminent note, and familiarly known to every Christian, being al-

* T. viii. p. 245, F., cited by Hopkins, vol. ii. p. 220.
† Contra lit. Petilian, l. ii. N. 87.

leged by their pastors and teachers, as an express and undoubted prophecy of the Christian sacrifice, or solemn worship in the Eucharist, taught by our Blessed Saviour unto His disciples, to be observed of all that should believe in His name; and this so generally and grantedly, as could never have been, at least so early, unless they had learned thus to apply it by tradition from the Apostles." Overall, with whose words they also furnish me, says in reference to this prediction, and that of the Psalmist concerning Melchisedech: "both which the ancient fathers, with one consent, understood of the sacrifice of the Eucharist, and the priests of the Gospel."* Hickes observes: "The ancients always spoke of the Eucharist as the sacrifice of oblation of the Gentiles, in opposition to those of the Jews, when they argued against them from the prophecy of Malachi."†

Dr. Milner remarks, that "the Church of England has priests but no sacrifice, altars but no victim, an essential consecration of the sacramental elements, without even the least effect upon the elements." This you attempt to disprove, by a learned disquisition on the classical and scriptural Greek terms, ἱερευς and πρεσβύτερος, but the shortest and most effectual way to destroy the alleged inconsistencies, is to avow that you have neither priest nor altar. Hence,

* Tract N. 81. † Tracts, p. 258.

Bishop White, of Philadelphia, was opposed to the use of these terms: "It has been acknowledged," he says, "that the here supposed error concerning 'sacrifice,' 'altar,' and 'priest,' arose at an early period of the history of the Christian Church."* Archbishop Whately is notorious for the same opposition.†

When you call our doctrine "blasphemous presumption," you remind me of those of whom the Scripture speaks, "who blaspheme whatsoever things they know not." The consequences which you allege, do not flow from our belief. The priests are but the agents and ministers of Christ, doing what He commanded, and with trembling awe ministering in His presence.

It is easy to show that a true priesthood, with a real sacrifice, no other than the Body and Blood of Christ, was always recognized in the Christian Church, as it is still recognized by all the Oriental sects, as well as by Catholics. Archdeacon Wilberforce, in his learned work on the Eucharist, written before his submission to the Holy See, observes that "it may be asserted without fear of contradiction, that no doctrine of the Christian religion is affirmed with more unanimity by all ancient writers, than the truth

* Dissertation viii. of the Eucharist, by William White, p. 402.

† See the Priesthood in the Church, by William R. Whittingham, Bishop of Maryland, p. 5.

of the Eucharistic sacrifice."* This he proves by passages from St. Clement, St. Ignatius, Justin Martyr, St. Irenæus, St. Cyprian, St. Augustin, and by the ancient Liturgies. "The judgment of the Church to the time of the Council of Chalcedon, may be expressed in the following assertions: "First,—The thing offered in the Holy Eucharist, is affirmed in express terms to be the Body of Christ." "Secondly,—The sacrifice offered in the Holy Eucharist is affirmed not to be anything superadded to that on the Cross, nor yet a repetition of it." "Thirdly,—The victim offered in the Holy Eucharist, was said to be identical with Him who offered it." "Fourthly,—It was the habitual custom of ancient writers to speak of the sacrifice of the Holy Eucharist as awful, august, and terrible." "Fifthly,—They speak of the sacrifice of the Holy Eucharist, as truly efficacious for the obtaining of all those things which are the subject-matter of prayer and of intercession." "Sixthly,—The sacrifice of the Holy Eucharist is declared to have been that which the Jewish ordinances were intended to typify." "Seventhly,—But the sacrifice of the Holy Eucharist is said to differ from those of the law, in that the latter were only a shadow, while the former is a reality." "Eighthly,—To offer the sacrifice of the Holy Eucharist, is declared to be an especial office, committed to the Apostles and their successors."† I shall not trouble you,

* The Holy Eucharist, ch. xi. p. 318. † Ibidem.

Right Reverend Sir, with the detailed proofs of each assertion furnished by the illustrious author; but if you will condescend to read them, I have some hope that you will repent having branded our doctrine with the characters of presumption and blasphemy.

The loss of the Christian priesthood is the greatest calamity which has befallen the Church of England. In separating from the communion of the chief Bishop, the proud prince who swayed her destinies, fancied that he would preserve the hierarchy with its worship; but the penalty of revolt soon overtook the children of disobedience; and when the bold Elizabeth undertook to reconstruct the Church, she found herself obliged to supply by royal edicts and acts of Parliament, deficiencies in those who were to be the fathers of the new prelacy. I am quite willing that you should treat as fabulous the story of the Nag's head ordination, and that you should assume as proved the ordination of Barlow; but the total inattention to the sacrificial character of the priesthood, and to the Divine powers of the episcopate, in the forms adopted under Edward, and followed in the ordination of Matthew Parker, and of all English bishops and presbyters for more than a hundred years, convinces me that all real priestly character has vanished from your communion. Indeed, it is scarcely claimed. Bishop Whittingham, in his two sermons on the Priesthood, although stickling for the term, studiously avoids attributing to it the distinctive office of presenting a real sacrifice. You manifestly discard the idea. "Yet what a mockery," cries Archdeacon Wilberforce, "is a priestly commission which confers no powers, and a form of consecration whereby nothing is made holy?"* Thus you are destitute of all that antiquity judged essential to the Christian ministry. Very properly you have laid aside the vestments which were employed in the act of sacrifice, and although some would fain place your communion table where the altar once stood, yet the instincts of Protestantism prevent any general innovation of this kind, which might give a coloring of reality to that which is by your own avowal but the shadow: *magni nominis umbra.*

As you take occasion to rail at the practice of receiving a very small offering on occasion of celebrating Mass, I must remind you that it is a remnant of the ancient usage of making oblations of wine, flour, and other provisions at the time of the sacrifice. It is presented as a contribution towards the support of the priest,†

* Ibidem, p. 75.

† It was not thought unworthy of recording among the acts of piety that marked the childhood of St. Peter Damiani, that he made an offering of a small coin which came into his possession, to have Mass celebrated according to his intention. The act is an alms on the part of the donor, with the additional merit of being consecrated to the maintenance of Divine worship. It is not given as a price, or consideration.

on the principle of God's own ordinance, that "they who serve the altar should partake with the altar." You make a gross misstatement when you assert of our clergy: "They never perform those masses without the payment in money of a stipulated sum." Thousands of Masses are celebrated without any offering whatever being made. All bargaining is strictly forbidden. The Church, in allowing us to receive the free contributions of the faithful, for our necessary support, has cautiously guarded against abuses by strict enactments, charging her ministers, as they have gratuitously received, to give also gratuitously.

LETTER VIII.

On Communion under One Kind.

Right Reverend Sir:

WHILST you deny the real Presence of the Body and Blood of our Lord in the Eucharist, and the true sacrifice of our altars, I cannot hope to convince you of the reasonableness of our discipline in administering it under one kind. This custom was introduced, indeed, by force of circumstances, not by any positive enactment; but it has been maintained especially with a view to oppose the grievous error which regards the sacrament as mere bread and wine. The Church believing the Body and Blood of Christ to be truly present, and inseparably united, holds that both are received, even when one kind only is taken. Although the custom of communicating under both kinds still continues among the Greeks, they believe with us that the Body and Blood of Christ are contained under each form, and even under each separate particle. In the Council of Jerusalem, A. D., 1672, they declared: "We believe that in every portion, even to the minutest subdivision, of the bread and wine after they have been changed, are contained not any separate part of the Body and Blood of the Lord, but the Body of Christ is always whole and one in all its parts; and the Lord Jesus is present in His substance, that is, with His Soul and Divinity, as perfect God and perfect man."* Why we should adhere to this usage of communion under one kind in apparent opposition to the original institution, perplexes the superficial observer; but Providence has so directed that in this respect, as well as in regard to baptism, we may not appeal to the mere letter of Scripture against the teaching and practice of those to whom Christ committed the dispensation of the sacraments. Were each one to judge of the mode of baptizing by the scriptural statement of the baptism which our Lord received, or of the manner of giving the Eucharist by the transactions of the supper-room, we should change the place and mode of baptism, and the time and all the circumstances of the Eucharistic celebration. To be consistent, you should in all matters which regard the administration of both sacraments defer to the authority of the Church.

Our Lord in the Eucharist has given us a sacrifice, as well as sacrament, and as the former implies the immolation of a victim, the separate

* Quoted by Wilberforce on the Eucharist, ch. iii. § iii. This is translated from the Russ version. Neal's Introd. p. 1155. The Greek is in Harduin, xi. p. 254.

consecration of the bread and wine is directed to present the Body and Blood separately, as they were offered on the cross, the Body being stretched upon it, while the Blood streamed from the veins. In this consists the mystical sacrifice of our altars; for which reason the reception of both kinds is regarded as appertaining to its consummation, and is enjoined on the celebrant. The communicants are made partakers of both the Body and the Blood under either kind, because the Blood is not now actually separated from the Body, and therefore they enjoy the full benefit of the sacrament. They are under no necessity of receiving both, because it does not devolve on them to consummate the sacrifice. For many ages it was generally allowed to receive both; but liberty was given to receive either alone, when a just cause existed, as in times of persecution, and in sickness. The occurrence of serious accidents, whilst the sacred cup was handed from lip to lip, was one of the chief occasions of introducing the custom of receiving under the species of bread only. No divine command can be shown to receive both, since the words, "Drink ye all of this," were addressed to the Apostles, and by them fulfilled at the moment: "and they all drank of it." There is an obvious reason, why they should receive both on that solemn occasion, when they were associated to the priesthood of

Christ, to be ever afterwards His agents in the act of sacrifice.

You admit that the English Parliament, as well as Calvin, allow the partaking of the bread without the wine, in cases of necessity; but you deny that this implies anything favorable to our discipline. Yet is it not evidence that the Church of England does not regard both elements as absolutely essential?

The manner of administering the sacraments appertains to discipline, and is consequently subject to the discretionary power of the Church, which regulates it according to circumstances, in various places, or at various periods. The Eucharist was given under both elements, for nearly twelve centuries, which is still the practice of the Eastern churches. Throughout the West, it is given only under the species of bread, which usage was gradually introduced from a variety of causes, some of which have been specified above, and for about six hundred years it has been fully established.

St. Leo complained of the Manicheans, who abstained from the sacred cup, regarding wine as a production of the evil principle. They also disbelieved the reality of the sufferings of Christ, and were therefore opposed to the receiving of the Blood, which the faithful believed to be given in the mystery. In order to discover and separate them from the faithful, Pope Gelasius ordered that all should receive under both kinds.

You remark, that the established rule was to give both the species to the laity. Of this there is no dispute; but it was left free to receive under both, until the errors of these secret heretics rendered it advisable to enforce their reception. When that cause ceased to exist, it was again left optional, and the custom of receiving only in one kind at length prevailed. Archdeacon Wilberforce observes, that "both kinds were held to communicate one gift, which was supposed to be imparted perfectly through every portion of either element." In proof, he quotes St. Cyril, of Alexandria: "For as St. Paul says, 'A little leaven leaveneth the whole lump,' so the very smallest portion of the Eucharist transfuses our whole body into itself, and fills us with its own energy, and thus Christ comes to exist in us, and we in him."* He also states the custom of bishops sending the Eucharist one to another, and of deacons carrying it to the sick, of hermits keeping it in their cells, and of the faithful generally having it in times of persecution, in all which circumstances one kind only was generally received.† "The mention of bread only, when the holy Eucharist was received in private houses, leads to the conclusion that it was partaken in that kind alone. The story of Serapion, as related by Eusebius, shows that this was sup-

* In Joan, vi. 57, vol. iv. p. 365.

† Wilberforce on the Eucharist, ch. iii. s. 111.

posed sufficient in the case of the sick, and from a circumstance recorded by St. Cyprian, we learn that infants were communicated under the other kind only."*

Your proof, from the Council of Chalcedon, is superfluous, as regards the acknowledged usage. Your commentary is remarkable. The text says, "That those to whom they gave the sacred Body, made signs and went out, because the Blood was wanting;" you add: "This clearly shows that the people not only received the wine, but expected to be supplied well and liberally."†

The practice reproved by the Council of Braga (Bracara), is still found among the Greeks, who, on some occasions, dip the host in the chalice, and give it thence to the communicant. The Council of Clermont, in the canon given by you, plainly held the mystery as we hold it, to be the Body and Blood of Christ, and allowed communion under one kind in cases of necessity, or when caution recommended it. The Bishop of Salisbury, in his constitution, which you recite, alludes to the general usage, and bears testimony to the truth of Christ's Body and Blood. The precautions against accidents and the painful prescriptions to remedy them, show that the faith of those times was identical with our own.

* Wilberforce on the Eucharist, p. 72. † Vol. ii. p. 187.

LETTER IX.

On Penance.

RIGHT REVEREND SIR:

OF the established Church of England and the Catholic Church you say: "Both churches agree in the necessity of the repentance of sin, confession of sin, and absolution from sin, without which (the case of infants alone excepted) there can be no salvation." I did not before imagine that we harmonized so far: but why any mention should be made of infants, where actual sin is in question, I am at a loss to understand.

You deny our right to change the scriptural term "repentance" into "penance." The New Testament was written in Greek; neither term occurs in the original text. You think that the Greek should be rendered "repentance." By closer observation, you will find that "penance" is the English modification of the Latin *pœnitentia*, and that "agere pœnitentiam" is an elegant as well as correct translation of μετανοειν. But it is useless to detain our readers with a verbal criticism, since usage determines the force of words. When the ancient Latin translation was made, there could be no motive for misrepresenting the text, as the present controversies had no existence. The Rhemish translators scrupulously adhered to the Latin.

You are mistaken in stating that all the circumstances of sin must be confessed. No circumstance need be stated that does not aggravate the guilt of the sinner; nay, divines more generally hold, that such circumstances only as change the character of the sin need be specified. We take great care to guard penitents against entering into any unnecessary details, particularly such as might point to individuals, and prejudice character. In stating that "all are forced to come before a private tribunal of compulsory judgment," you may lead some to suppose that other means are employed besides an appeal to conscience, under a threat of forfeiting the communion of the Church, which penalty is rarely inflicted. In designating it private, you may be thought to insinuate that the place of receiving confessions is such, especially as your book abounds with the basest insinuations; but the Ritual directs that confessionals be erected in the public church. The circumstances of a missionary country led in the beginning to the practice of hearing confessions in rooms, in which the sacrifice itself was also offered, or which immediately adjoined the church; but measures have been adopted by the councils to enforce conformity to the general discipline. You insist that "Rome demands secrecy, not only from the priest, but also from the penitent; so that if the priest should err, the people have no remedy." In this you are mistaken. Secrecy is recommended, that the priest may not suffer for advice conscientiously given for the guidance of his penitent; but if he impose unreasonable burdens, or in any way misdirect, or aggrieve, full liberty is enjoyed to have recourse to any other confessor; and even independently of any grievance, the change of confessors is unrestricted. In case of any attempt to abuse the ministry, even in the most indirect way, the penitent is bound to denounce him to his ecclesiastical superior.

You are mistaken in supposing that the Council of Trent declared that attrition is sufficient to insure pardon in the sacrament of penance. The term designedly employed is "disponit," which means only that it is a disposition for pardon, without determining its sufficiency. You must, however, have a very erroneous idea of the meaning which we attach to the word "attrition." It implies a hatred and detestation of sin, on account of its baseness, and of the punishments which God justly inflicts on the sinner. It is not a mere slavish fear of punishment, with a continued affection to sin, since such a disposition could not serve for our justification. Contrition springing from the love of God is strongly recommended in the Ritual; which the confessor accordingly endeavors to excite; but whenever he is assured that the penitent is truly sorry for having sinned, and determined to shun it for the time to come, he may feel encouraged to absolve him, as having the necessary disposition. Chillingworth, whose fame you are said to rival, says: "Though He (God), like best the bright flaming holocaust of love, yet He rejects not, He quenches not the smoking flax of that repentance, if it be true and effectual, which proceeds from hope and fear."*

Of the casting oneself down at the feet of the confessor, the Ritual says nothing. The expression is used in some prayer-books to mark the humility with which the penitent should kneel in the confessional, which Tertullian declared in similar terms: "advolvi presbyteris." It is never done literally.

You carp at our form of absolution, because it is absolute, not deprecatory, as in some ancient rituals; but you should reflect that the same form is still retained in the English Book of Common Prayer, which, however, the American Episcopal Convention has abandoned. This is one of the striking points of difference between you and the Church of England. She prescribes absolution to be given before communion, to individuals whose consciences prompt them to seek its benefit, and she directs the

* "The Religion of Protestants a sure Way to Salvation," ch. i.

minister to exhort the dying to confess whatever burdens his conscience, and to absolve him. To deny the power of forgiveness is, as Bishop Pearson avows, the heresy of Novatian.* Yet you only retain in the morning service a form of supplication, or general declaration that those who repent will be forgiven, not venturing to exercise real power and authority to forgive sins in the name of Christ, although in the form of ordination it is implied. Such of your ministers as think that they ought to exercise it, expose themselves to be called to answer before their Bishop and the Standing Committee, on suspicion of Popery, as I believe took place a few years ago in Boston.

All you say about "forcing all to come up, whether willing or unwilling, and bare their inmost thoughts to our inspection," is imaginary. No one confesses except of his own free will, and as far as he pleases. He is bound to confess his sins, but not mere temptations, to which he has given no consent, or occasion; much less such thoughts, views, or intentions, as involve no moral guilt.

When St. Paul charged Timothy to rebuke them that sin before all, he spoke of public and scandalous delinquents, not of the frail penitent who seeks a remedy for secret faults. In the same spirit, the Council of Trent directs that open delinquents should be publicly reproved;

* Exposition of the Creed, art. ix.

but the humble and contrite need milder treatment. You rail against the Council of Lateran as having dispensed virtually with the apostolic rule of public discipline; yet its enactment enforcing the duty of confession implied no such dispensation. It was directed to awaken sinners to repentance, and effect their reformation, which needs their own free return to duty.

The testimonies of the fathers are disposed of by you very readily. Tertullian advises the sinner who shrinks from confession, to "think of hell, whose fires confession extinguishes."* You ask me; "How does this show whether the confession was to God, or to the priest; in public, or in private; voluntary, or enforced?"† He certainly does not mean secret confession to God, since he represents sinners as delaying it through false shame and unwillingness to expose their frailty. He might be supposed to urge public confession, as he details many penitential exercises; but that private confession is specially meant, appears from the penitents casting themselves at the feet of the priests, doubtless to obtain reconciliation through their ministry. You, however, have neither private nor public confession, and you deny the necessity of either.

Tertullian, you observe, speaks of penitence as only allowed once, which you rightly understand of public penance; but you cannot mean to ex-

* L. de pœnit. c. ix. † Vol. ii. p. 250.

clude the penitent from divine mercy, whenever he returns to God with all his heart, and in deep affliction of soul. As public penance was enjoined chiefly for notorious and heinous crimes, and as it was accompanied with much solemnity, it was proper that it should not be trifled with by repetition. Secret sins had always a remedy in private confession, which also embraced sins that were public; but as the discipline then established required public penance for these, it was wisely prescribed that in case of relapse, the delinquent should not again enter on the penitential course, but be left to mourn and repair his fall privately.

The acts of penance are noted by Tertullian in his very graphic description. The penitent, he says, "falls down before the priests, and embraces the knees of those who are the beloved of God," (according to another reading, kneels at the altars of God), "enjoining on all the brethren the commission to intercede in his behalf." The first clause is naturally referred to sacramental confession; the second, if we retain your reading, "charis Dei," may have the same meaning; the last manifestly implies entreaties addressed to the faithful by penitents, asking their intercession with the Church for their speedy restoration to communion, or with God for their pardon. Your inference that "there was no secrecy, no private tribunal of the priest alone," is not justified by the text.

Origen advises the penitent to look round diligently, and select a confessor, as he would a physician.* You infer thence, that he regarded confession as a mere matter of expediency. This consequence does not follow; since it is necessary in serious illness to have a physician, although a choice is not denied us. You contrast the liberty which Origen allows with the law of Lateran, which obliges each one to confess to his own parish priest. The law, however, is not quite so stringent, since there is an alternative, "or to another priest by his leave." Besides, custom has so mitigated it, that it is sufficient to confess to any approved priest. St. Francis De Sales gives the same advice as Origen, urging those who aspire to perfection, to pray for a safe guide, and choose a confessor of known piety and prudence. Eusebius, who belongs rather to the fourth century than to the third, commends "confession not to men, but to God, who searches the heart;"† but this does not exclude sacramental confession, which has always been regarded as made to God, not to man, who is merely His minister. It is certain that public confession was extolled and practised, and that it also was considered as made to God, because it proceeded from motives of religion.

St. Athanasius, whom you quote, says that "not to judge our neighbor gives pardon for all

* Hom. ii. in Ps. xxxvii.

† Comm. in Ps. p. 608.

sins;"* but this means only that it disposes us to obtain their pardon, our Lord having said, "Judge not, and ye shall not be judged." Such language does not preclude the necessity of employing the means which God has appointed for securing forgiveness. In like manner, when he assigns to the sinner as a test for ascertaining whether he has recovered the grace of God, the familiarity in prayer, by which his soul communes with the Creator,† he is only pointing to a token that may afford reasonable confidence to the penitent. He is not treating of the mode of reconciliation.

St. Basil, you observe, prescribes to his monks confession as an exercise of religious discipline. The terms are general and applicable to all, although the duty is specially inculcated to the monks in the Rule: "it is necessary to confess our sins to those who are intrusted with the dispensation of the mysteries of God."‡ He uses the comparison, which Tertullian and Origen had already employed, of the physician, to whom we should disclose our most secret maladies and infirmities. In addressing the people at large, he says: "Have you committed a great and grievous sin? You have need of much confession and bitter tears."§

* Op. t. ii. p. 366, qu. 76. † Ib. qu. 77.

‡ In Reg. brev. resp. ad qu. 288.

§ Hom. in hæc verba: "Attende tibi ipsi."

St. Ambrose is praised for his sympathy with his penitents, since he wept over their transgressions, and disclosed them to no one but to God. This, you observe, would be unnoticed, if he were bound to entire secrecy, which we hold to be a necessary duty of the confessor. There is some justice in this remark; but may not his biographer, St. Paulinus, refer to his extreme caution never to speak, even in general terms, of what came to his knowledge through the confessional? The strictest divines admit that it involves no breach of the sacramental seal to speak in this way, when there is no danger whatever of suspicion lighting on the penitent; yet it is seldom that such a practice is free from all objections, so that a confessor is worthy of praise, who never in any way alludes to any class of sins which have thus come to his knowledge.

St. Augustin, you say, speaks of public penance, when he forbids the sinner to flatter himself that he can obtain Divine mercy by private penance. Yet his words are such as might be addressed to you, or any other Protestant who relies on the sufficiency of confession to God alone. "Let no one say to himself: I do penance secretly; I do it before God; God, who is to pardon me, knows the sentiments of my heart." To this specious reasoning against the necessity of applying for pardon to the ministers of religion, St. Augustin replies: "Then it has been said to no purpose, 'What ye shall loose on earth shall be loosed also in heaven.' Then the keys have been given to the Church of God in vain! We make void the Gospel; we make void the words of Christ."* He distinctly states the duty of private confession in the third passage, which you yourself quote. Speaking of one who is conscious of deadly sins against the Decalogue, he says: "Being bound, therefore, by the chains of those deadly sins, ... let him come to the prelates, by whom the keys of the Church are applied, and let him accept the mode of his satisfaction, and as it were already beginning to act as a devoted child, keeping the order that should exist between the members of the same mother, let him learn from those who preside over the administration of the sacraments, the manner in which he must satisfy, so that, being devout and suppliant in offering the sacrifice of a sorrowful heart, he may do what not only shall be profitable to his own salvation, but shall also serve as an example for others. So that, if his sin be not merely to his own grievous injury, but is likewise a cause of great scandal to others, and if it shall seem expedient for the good of the Church, in the judgment of the Bishop, let him not refuse to do penance in the presence of

* Serm. cccxcii.

many, or even of all the people; let him not resist, nor through shame, add inflammation to the mortal and deadly wound."* The private disclosure of sin to the prelate, was necessary to determine whether its public acknowledgment was necessary or proper.

The principle of conduct which Augustin lays down in the other passage which you cite, harmonizes perfectly with our rules: "We cannot prohibit any one from the communion (although this prohibition is not yet mortal, but medicinal), unless he be accused and convicted, either by his own voluntary confession, or by some secular or ecclesiastical judgment."† Confession is left entirely to the conscience of the individual. All who present themselves for communion are deemed worthy, unless some flagrant crime show the contrary.

The daily medicine of prayer is available for venial sins, as Augustin teaches. We ask forgiveness before communion, that we may be purified from every slight stain, and rendered worthy of the Divine Gift. Confession of slight sins is not required by the divine law, although it is constantly practised.‡

The practice of confession in the second century is attested by St. Irenæus, who speaks of women deluded by a sectary of the name of

* Serm. cccli. alias L. c. 4. † Ibidem.

‡ Tom. v. Op. p. 68. Sermo de decem chordis. A.

Mark, who, on their return to the faith, confessed that they had been seduced and corrupted by him.* It is also attested by the ancient fathers generally; and it is invincibly established by the fact that the practice has come down in the Church; since it never could have been introduced after the days of the Apostles, for nothing less than a divine command promulgated by them, could have established an observance so difficult.

Fleury, your guide, states indeed that the first instance he has met with of confession being enjoined, is in the constitutions of St. Chrodegang, Bishop of Metz, in the year 763, who required his priests to confess to him twice a year, at stated periods, under penalty of flagellation, if they failed, or if they withheld any grievous fault. The terms and the penalty show that this was a monastic regulation, for in that age, when the manners of men were not as yet free from traces of their barbarous ancestors, the fierce Northmen, the whip was sometimes a necessary aid in preserving discipline. At other times of the year confession might be made by the members of that institute to a priest delegated by the Superior. The regulations which St. Chrodegang made were presented by him as a mitigation of the stricter rule of ancient monasteries, which required their inmates to disclose all their inmost thoughts.

* L. i. ad. hær. ix.

The first general law requiring confession was passed in the fourth Council of Lateran, whose enactments you bring under notice very frequently. But the divine law was always recognized, which obliges all sinners to confess their sins, that the power of loosing and binding may be discreetly and effectually exercised in their behalf. As in the apostolic age, the faithful came confessing their deeds and parting with the superstitious books which in their previous ignorance they had used, so in every succeeding age, they continued to practise confession, although no ecclesiastical enactment enforced that duty. In the thirteenth century it was found necessary to urge it under the severest penalty that the Church can inflict; but as the duty was acknowledged by all, nothing was said to prove it.

"Dr. Milner," you say, "has the effrontery to tell his readers that all this is in accordance with the fathers." I leave the readers to say who has effrontery.

A certain penitential canon prescribed that one who could not fast on bread and water should sing fifty psalms on his knees in the church for one day of fasting, and feed one poor man for that day. The Council of Worms, in 1022, commuted the obligation of singing psalms for a hundred genuflexions, and allowed money to be given instead of actually feeding the poor man. You have put this in capitals, translating "*se racheter par argent*" by REDEEM THEMSELVES FOR MONEY, which is rather an equivocal expression. I take leave to add the remarks of Fleury, which you have omitted: "It is proper to observe that this exemption from penance was only for such as could not possibly perform it as prescribed, and that this impossibility was not deemed a reason for an absolute dispensation, but merely for a commutation, so that the sinner might punish himself as far as in his power."* The money was not given *to redeem themselves*, but to be employed in the feeding of the poor, and thus to secure exemption from the literal compliance with the canon. I hope this does not strike you as simoniacal. The penitential discipline of that age, either in its strict form or as modified by dispensation, will scarcely gain your approval.

You reject, apparently on the authority of Fleury, the principle that one may satisfy for another; but perhaps you misunderstand your author, as well as the application of the principle. The Church certainly may remit something of her penitential discipline, in regard to the atonement or satisfaction offered by one of her children for a frail brother, when he seeks reconciliation with a contrite heart. On that principle, those who had suffered persecution in the age of St. Cyprian, pleaded effectually in behalf of

* Vol. xii. l. lviii. an. 1022.

apostates, who returned penitent to the Church. God sent the friends of Job to seek his prayers, promising to accept them in their behalf. Christ had regard to the faith of those who brought the palsied man to him. St. Paul supplied in his flesh for the body of the faithful what was wanting to secure to them the application of the sufferings of Christ. This vicarious expiation is, of course, unavailing to the sinner who remains obstinately attached to crime; but it is profitable to the penitent, through the merits of our Redeemer.

Your diligence in tracing the decline of penitential discipline, and your apparent zeal for the system of public penance, might lead some to suppose that it was still preserved in your communion; whilst the truth is, that public and private penance is equally discarded; fasting and all commutation for it are ignored; penance is rejected as an unscriptural term; and the sinner is flattered with the belief that he can obtain pardon by his secret repentance, without recourse to any ecclesiastical authority, the testimony and practice of all antiquity to the contrary notwithstanding.

Your statistics in regard to the confessional are amusingly erroneous. We hear confessions not during one week only in the year, but every day, and often for hours together. The time occupied with each penitent is generally very short, for confession is not a circumstantial detail of events. The sinner, in a few brief words, recounts his prevarications, avoiding all unnecessary specifications, and the priest, after brief admonitions and injunctions, when satisfied of his true sorrow, pronounces him absolved. This may appear to you to afford no evidence of the disposition of the sinner; but an experienced physician soon discovers the disease and applies the remedy. You suppose that we give more time to converts, to enable them to appreciate the consolations of the confessional. They are treated like all others, according to the state of their consciences. Every penitent, by his own statements, determines the amount of time to be employed, the inquiries to be made, the advice to be given, the obligations to be imposed. It is impossible for you, sir, to appreciate this ministry; but thousands who daily experience its advantages, can attest that by it they have been reclaimed from vice, and strengthened and directed in the path of virtue. It affords relief to the despondent sinner; it encourages the timid, it guides the unwary. It wipes away tears of bitterness, that might end in despair; it dissolves enmities; it heals rankling wounds; it covers shame, that exposed might lead to self-destruction; it saves from unperceived precipices; it breaks chains forged by long habits of vice; it snatches from the plunderer his prey, and gives it back to the despoiled owner; it disarms the conspirator, and throws a shield around the unprotected; it raises the sinner from death to life. Those who know human weakness, and all the mental anguish that in some form or other, distresses almost every individual of the human family, may conceive something of the advantages of an institution which inspires entire confidence, and secures advice and consolation in the most afflicting circumstances. The confessor does not mock the sorrow of his penitent, or reproach him with his misfortunes. He bids him hope, when all around have abandoned him, and as soon as he discovers that his compunction is deep and effectual, he says to him, in the spirit of Him who does not break the bruised reed, "Son, be of good heart: thy sins are forgiven thee." It may be impossible to restore the unhappy offender to his place in society, even to the affection of a fond parent, whose feelings have been outraged; or to rescue him from the arm of the law, which is outstretched to inflict its severest penalty; but in the name of Him who came into this world to save sinners, the priest of God assures him of pardon and salvation.

LETTER X.

On Purgatory.

RIGHT REVEREND SIR:

ALTHOUGH Dr. Milner distinctly stated that Catholic faith does not determine the nature of the punishment endured in Purgatory, still you maintain it to be fire, and accuse him of equivocating, because he said that we are not bound to believe it to be *material* fire. He was above all such quibbles. You ascribe to us interested motives for the maintenance of this doctrine: "Masses for the dead are of far more pecuniary value than Masses for the living." Not so; the same small offering is allowed for both, and is often given to the first beggar that solicits our charity.

You meet the first proof from the second book of the Macchabees, by denying the canonical authority of the book. It is enough for me to remind you that Beveridge acknowledges that these books were spoken of by St. Cyprian, and before him by Origen, precisely in the same manner as the books now received by all: "Since Cyprian cites those books among the canonical in the same breath, in the same series, without any distinction whatever, it is manifest that the Catholic Church of that age was wont to count them among the canonical books, especially since Origen also adds τὰ Μακκαβαϊκὰ to the books delivered by the Jewish Church to the Christian."* Further, you object that it proves too much, since those slain "were cut off for the crime of idolatry, and died in mortal sin." It does not appear that they worshipped the idols, but that they seized on donaries of the idols, contrary to the law, by which transgression they drew down vengeance on themselves. It was of itself a grievous sin; but Judas may have hoped that some acted in ignorance, or repented in death, and found mercy. You conjecture that the sacrifices were offered for the living, to reconcile God to them. The text says directly the contrary, and adds that Judas thought "well and religiously of the resurrection;" and infers "it is therefore a holy and wholesome thought to pray for the dead, that they may be loosed from their sins." The Greek says that he made an expiation for those who had died περὶ τῶν τεθνηκοτων.†

I will not discuss with you the obscure passage of St. Paul, respecting those who were baptized for the dead. If you can explain it satisfactorily in a different way from Dr. Milner,

* Codex Can. Prim. Eccl. l. 2, c. ix.

† 2 Mac. xii.

you will have accomplished what learned interpreters have often tried unsuccessfully.

You admit an intermediate state, without caring to define its character, and you allow Dr. Milner's application to it of two scriptural testimonies, Luke xvi. 22, 1 Peter iii. 9. His interpretation of the prison, from which there is no liberation until the last farthing is paid (Luke xii. 59), does not please you, because souls in Purgatory can do nothing to satisfy Divine justice; but their endurance is accepted, and the prayers of the Church may avail them, so that their debt may be discharged.

The inference drawn from Matt. xii. 32, that some sins may be forgiven hereafter, whilst the sin against the Holy Ghost shall never be forgiven, appears to you to force heretical doctrine on the Saviour Himself; inasmuch as no sin is forgiven in Purgatory, but punishment is endured for sins already forgiven. By reading our divines more attentively, you will perceive that we hold that venial sins are forgiven in that state, so that there is no foundation for your charge.

The various scriptural facts brought forward by Dr. Milner, namely, the punishment of death inflicted on our first parents, though penitent, the punishment of the Israelites, and of David after his sin was forgiven, were intended to prove that God often visits with temporal chastisements, sinners whose guilt He has pardoned; which point they fully establish. The fathers whom you quote, Irenæus, Tertullian, and Ambrose, seem to affirm that all souls, even those of the Saints, pass to the region in which the departed spirits were before the coming of our Saviour, and remain there to the Day of Judgment. Other passages, however, occur in their writings, especially in those of St. Ambrose, which are more in harmony with general tradition, and the Divine Scriptures, and with that doctrine which the Church has sealed with her solemn definition. Whatever may have been their individual sentiments, nothing said by them clashes with the doctrine of a middle state, in which souls are detained for slighter sins.

The observations of the Benedictine editors of St. Ambrose, to which you refer, are restricted by themselves to matters not then defined by the Church. They regard certain expressions and views, which some fathers put forward concerning the state of just souls before the final judgment, but which in other passages of their writings they modified or corrected, by adhering more closely to the general teaching of their predecessors. This does not imply any uncertainty as to the intermediate state, which we style Purgatory, since their language on this subject is sufficiently definite, and the usage of praying for the dead, which even Calvin admits to be very ancient,* is an evidence of the tradition that there is a state of departed souls, to

* In Acta Ap. c. xv. 10.

whom prayer may be beneficial. "Not without good reason," says St. Chrysostom, "it was ordained by the Apostles that mention should be made of the dead in the tremendous mysteries, because they knew that these would receive great benefit from it."* The sequel of this passage, which you give, does not weaken its force. Deceased catechumens were not included in the solemn prayers of the liturgy, because they had died without partaking of the communion of the Church; but as hope was cherished that their desire and disposition were acceptable to God, almsgiving was recommended, that it might be profitable to them, through Divine mercy, since good works, as well as prayer, may be offered for the departed. St. Chrysostom remarks that as we pray for the worst of living men, so we may pray for the departed, whose actual condition we know not.

The passages from the ancient Liturgies contain a commemoration of the Blessed Virgin and Saints, intended to express our communion with them, and that they have been saved by the merits of Christ, our victim. The words which follow remove all antiquity, since the priest asks, "that we may be helped by their intercessions." St. Augustin remarks, that "it is an insult to a martyr to pray in his behalf, for we ought rather to commend ourselves to his prayers.†"

* Hom. xxix. ad pop. Antioch. † Serm. xvii. de verbis Apostoli.

The testimony of Tertullian is admitted by you as proving the general custom of praying for the dead, since the pious widow "prays for the soul of her husband, and begs refreshment for him." He declares "*oblationes pro defunctis*" to be a stated part of "Christian worship," as Archdeacon Wilberforce avows.* Your explanation of the text of St. Cyprian, as marking the difference between public penitents, and the faithful who had not fallen in persecution, is ingenious. "It is one thing," says this father, "to stand for pardon (*ad veniam stare*), another to attain to glory; one thing to be sent to prison, not to go thence till the last farthing is paid, another to receive immediately the reward of faith and virtue; one thing to suffer lengthened torments for sin, and to be cleansed and purged a long time by fire (*emundari et purgari diu igne*), another to have cleansed away all sins by suffering," namely, by martyrdom. You explain *standing* as referring to the posture of penitents "in the outward porch of the church;" *to be sent to prison*, as meaning to be put on penance; to remain there until the last farthing is paid, by undergoing its full infliction; and *to be cleansed and purged a long time in the fire*, as implying long and severe penance. The passage which immediately follows, entirely upsets this fanciful interpretation: "It is one thing to be in suspense

* The Doctrine of the Holy Eucharist, p. 325.

as to the sentence of the Lord until the Day of Judgment, another to be immediately crowned by the Lord."* In this letter he maintains the propriety of pardoning and admitting to communion in death, repentant apostates, and undertakes to solve the objection of those, who thought that such indulgence would take away every incentive to fidelity and martyrdom. He observes that the pardon given to repentant adulterers did not cause the abandonment of holy virginity. Then he proceeds to show, that the penitent is not put on a level with the martyr in the Divine judgment, since he is kept in a state of suspense and suffering, whilst the martyr is immediately crowned with glory. St. Cyprian intimates that this state continues even to the last judgment. His work, addressed to Demetrian, a heathen, who by calumnies attacked Christianity, contains nothing inconsistent with what has just been stated. At its close, he tells him to be converted in time to the true God, for that at the Day of Judgment, repentance and entreaty will be fruitless. Whilst life lasts, penance is never too late. Even in death, mercy is granted to him who implores the only true God with faith, confessing Him, and asking pardon. In stating that the convert from heathenism at the very hour of death passes to immortality,† St. Cyprian doubtless relied on the grace of baptism, which,

* Ep. lii. ad Antonian. † L. ad Demetrian.

as we also hold, conveys entire pardon; for "there is no longer any condemnation to those who are in Christ Jesus." This case is very different from that of the penitent apostate, whose state of suspense and suffering is elsewhere depicted.

In his book on those who had fallen, St. Cyprian exhorts to repentance, confession, and satisfaction, whilst life remains, as after death there is no room for any exercise of salutary compunction. This perfectly accords with the Catholic teaching.

St. Augustin prayed for the soul of his mother Monica, conformably to her request, but you think that his conduct was the result of his feelings rather than of his theology, which, indeed, is contrary to his own express testimony. However, you admit that traces of our doctrine are found in his writings. He does not reject the sentiment of those who understand the Apostle (Cor. iii. 13), as intimating that imperfect souls suffer a certain punishment of fire until the day of the resurrection; because it is perhaps true; "That some of the faithful are saved through a certain purgatorial fire, more slowly or more speedily, according to their greater or less love for perishable goods, may be either found, or it may lie hidden." The doubt here implied seems to regard the punishment of actual fire, rather than the fact of such souls being in a state in which they need prayer for their relief. "It is not to be doubted," he says, as you yourself quote, "that the dead are aided by the prayers of the Holy Church, by the salutary sacrifice, and by alms-deeds offered for their souls, that the Lord may deal with them more mercifully than they have deserved. For, this custom delivered by the fathers, the whole Church observes, that for those who are deceased in the communion of the Body and Blood of Christ, when they are commemorated in their place at that sacrament, prayer is made, and for them also the sacrament is offered."* If you compare this passage with the decree of the Council of Trent,† you will find that it was present to the mind of the fathers. What St. Augustin adds, that these things are profitable only to such as have lived, or at least died in a manner to be capable of deriving benefit from them, is a Catholic principle.

No serious difficulty, as you imagine, was raised in the Council of Florence in regard to the nature of the punishments endured in Purgatory. At all events, we need not go beyond the definition in which the Greeks and Latins united. There is no evidence that this point was an occasion of the subsequent relapse of the Greeks, which regarded the procession from the Holy Ghost, and their subjection to the Roman See. The Tractarians observe: "They agreed together, as the Council shows, or at least, with

* T. V. op. p. 576, Serm. clxxii. § 2. † Sess. xxv.

the slightest difference, on the question in which we are concerned, while the subsequent resentment of the Greeks at home had little or no reference to it; and their agreement, under such circumstances, was only the more remarkable."*

You have then, Right Reverend Sir, the consent of the Greeks with the Catholic Church on the existence of an intermediate state, in which the departed benefit by the prayers of the living. The perpetual custom of offering prayer for them is a practical display of the faith which we cherish that they have slept in Christ, and are finally to repose with Him in glory. This usage, taken together with the public preaching of the Church, serves to shed light on certain passages of Scripture, which might otherwise be deemed not sufficiently explicit. You admit, and strive to explain away the usage, by making it common to all the departed, even to the greatest saints, but it is plainly directed to obtain refreshment and repose for the imperfect only.

The anecdote which you give us of our countryman, who asked you for ten dollars to give the priest for Masses, to get his wife's soul out of Purgatory, shows how largely he calculated on your prejudices. He meant, perhaps, to drink your health at your own expense, and treat his companions, whilst exulting in your gullibility; but he was justly disappointed by your discernment.

* Tract No. 79.

Prayer for the departed is one of those consoling practices of piety which the Reformers did not venture at once to discard, either, as you would say, perhaps, because they were still under Popish influences, or because they felt that they would provoke, unnecessarily, the popular indignation. The prayer which we use in the canon of the Mass was adopted in the first edition of the Book of Common Prayer, with some slight modification: "We commend unto Thy mercy, O Lord, all Thy servants which are departed hence from us with the sign of faith, and now do rest in the sleep of peace. Grant unto them, we beseech Thee, Thy mercy and everlasting peace, and that at the day of the general resurrection, we, and all they which be of the mystical body of Thy Son, may altogether be set on His right hand."* The words which follow "peace" are easily discernible as an addition to the prayer of the Missal. You appear not altogether opposed to this practice, but you do not advocate its revival. Yet you know it to come down from the earliest and purest period of antiquity.

* The two books of Common Prayer, compared. Oxford, 1841. pp. 296.

LETTER XI.

Indulgences.

RIGHT REVEREND SIR:

FLEURY states, as you remark, that the plenary indulgence was introduced by Pope Urban II. to favor the crusade, at the close of the eleventh century; but he adds that at all times the Church had allowed the bishops to remit a portion of the canonical penance. The complete remission of the whole, which he regarded as a relaxation of discipline, is what he alleges was first granted by Urban II. to the crusaders. By remarking that the indulgence was instead of wages to the soldiery, he does not mean that it was convertible into money. On the contrary, the crusaders not only served without pay, but even equipped and supported themselves, deeming it sufficient that they should gain the spiritual blessing. Indulgences were likewise granted to such as contributed to the expenses of these wars, because such generosity was deemed worthy of approval, and spiritual treasures were thought to be fitly distributed among those who had sacrificed their wealth for Christ. They were granted by Leo X. to such as contributed to the building of St. Peter's. As it was lawful to solicit the alms of the faithful throughout the world for this great work of general importance, so it was allowable to encourage it by the promise of spiritual treasures. There was nothing simoniacal, sacrilegious, or improper in thus employing the power of the Church in favor of penitent sinners. You accuse popes, cardinals, and bishops of it, as of a crime continued for four hundred years; and call it a bargain and sale. I see in it, in the abstract, nothing criminal, although abuses incidental to it led to the suppression of the office of Questors, or collectors of alms, by the Council of Trent.

The decree of this Council, which you recite, refers to the importunities and exaggerations of the collectors, in urging the faithful to give contributions for the objects for which the indulgences were proclaimed. They brand these abuses as *pravos quæstus*, which you translate *wicked merchandizings*. The abolition of that office took from the sectaries an abundant source of defamation. Yet, although no vestige of it remains, you insist that "indulgences are bought and sold as much as ever." They, sir, were never bought or sold; and if, at times, abuses grew out of the custom of connecting with them collections for objects of religion, charity, or public convenience, that custom has been abolished. You say that "the price of indulgences is a serious item of the priestly and the papal income," whilst in fact, nothing whatever comes to priest or Pope from their use or concession. You say: "I leave it to your skill in Roman casuistry to defend the veracity of your favorite in the best way you can." It is easy to defend one who speaks the truth, which the Catholic world can attest, but I know only one way by which your veracity can be defended, namely, that you make your statements in entire ignorance of the facts.

The argument drawn from the conduct of St. Paul towards the penitent Corinthian is not fairly met by you. "St. Paul gives directions concerning a single penitent, of whose case he was fully informed. The Pope issues millions of pardons to people of whom he knows nothing." The question now simply is, Did St. Paul free the penitent from further penance by authority received from Christ? If he did, he granted what is technically called an Indulgence. The Pope grants it in general terms to all, who, being penitent, comply with certain religious duties. The number of persons in favor of whom the power is exercised does not change its character. "St. Paul gives his judgment without money and without price. The Pope grants his Indulgence for a consideration." As you repeat this calumny, let me use your own words: "Which shall we most admire, the outrageous absurdity, or the cool effrontery of such an argument?"

The Jubilee, you allege, brings to Rome a vast amount of substantial treasure in return for the spiritual gift. In this you are mistaken; it brings nothing whatever. Although almsdeeds, with fasting and prayer, are usually prescribed on that occasion, the object of the alms and the amount are left to the discretion of the faithful. No portion of it, whatever, goes into the Roman treasury. The many indulgences specified in "True Piety" are to be gained by confession and communion, without almsgiving. You appeal to me as knowing that it is *a cash transaction*, since they cannot be had *without the money*.

I know no such thing. I know on the contrary that no money is given, or taken; and despising the quibble by which you say the people *give* the price, and the priest *gives* the indulgence, I pronounce your statement utterly false and groundless.

As to what is done in South America, your information can scarcely be relied on, since you are so grossly mistaken as to the usages which prevail around you. I am aware that in the dominions of Spain, a practice has existed which may give some coloring to your allegations. The Holy See was induced to grant certain privileges and exemptions, like those granted to the crusaders, whence it is styled *the Bull of the Crusade*, to persons contributing as alms a small sum, to a religious purpose, chiefly, I believe, the maintenance of missionaries in Jerusalem. Persons obtaining the certificate, or Bula, are dispensed with the obligation of abstinence, provided their physician and confessor deem it expedient; *con el consejo de los dos medicos spiritual y corporal.* Its chief design is to impose a fine, by way of commutation, on persons seeking to be dispensed from the Church laws, as is done by the Church of England in case of marriage licenses, and various other exemptions from law. It has proved, I believe, fatal to that portion of our discipline in the Spanish dominions; but it is not, after all, a sale of dispensations, or indulgences. I am happy to say that no such usage exists in the United States, or throughout the Church generally. In the reign of Edward VI. an Act was passed enjoining abstinence on fish-days, "as a mean to virtue, and to subdue men's bodies to their soul and spirit, and also to encourage the trade of fishing, and for saving of flesh; excepting such as should obtain the King's license;" for which, no doubt, some fees of office were required.

The treasure of the Church is a figurative expression, which marks the sources from which she draws in exercising her power. The merits of Christ are infinite; but the communion of the faithful is such that they also may benefit one another, by prayer, good works, or sufferings offered up one for the other. The excruciating torments endured by the martyrs, the extreme austerities of some penitents, the suffering of apostolic men in the propagation of the Gospel, may be profitable to the weaker members. The saints have, indeed, received a reward exceedingly great; their sufferings were momentary and light compared with the eternal weight of glory, with which they are crowned; yet their endurance may be advantageously pleaded before God to obtain for us some remission of the punishment due to our sins. It can only be offered through Christ our Lord, and through Him only can become available.

You accuse Dr. Milner of omitting to state that indulgences are designed to remit to the sinner the torments of Purgatory, after he shall have passed away from the Church on earth. They are directed to remit the canonical penance, which was enjoined to satisfy the justice of God, who often inflicts temporal punishments for sins whose guilt is forgiven. Dr. Milner expressly states that indulgences remit not only the canonical penance, but the corresponding punishment in the sight of God. In this sense, indulgences may preserve from purgatory; but they are not given to any one, to take effect after his death. Some are applicable to the souls in purgatory, inasmuch as the living who gain them, may offer them in behalf of the departed; but as the Church has no control over her departed children, they are not strictly effectual, but offered by way of suffrage, in the confidence that God will accept them.

LETTER XII.

Devotion to the Blessed Virgin.

RIGHT REVEREND SIR:

YOU charge Dr. Milner "with a shameful withholding of the real worship which the Church of Rome renders to the Virgin and the Saints;" and in order to make good this grave accusation, you give extracts from certain books of devotion in use among Catholics. As he, however, quoted the words of the Council of Trent, in proof of our principles, justice requires that the expressions and acts of devotion used by us should be explained in conformity with that standard. The passages which you quote from the popular prayer-book called "True Piety," when thus understood, contain nothing that is objectionable. They express great confidence in the prayers of the Blessed Virgin, as one most highly favored by Almighty God, and most dear to our Redeemer. I am surprised that you have not understood the addresses which are sometimes made to Him as the Infant Jesus. Dr. Pusey, in his treatise on baptism, admires the custom of the Church, by which she makes present to her children the various mysteries which she celebrates, as if they happened at the present time. Thus contemplating the Incarnation, the Christian adores the Divine Infant, calls on Him for mercy, and gives himself over to affections of gratitude and love. No one,—not even the most unlettered, imagines that He is still an Infant in the arms of His Mother. We know that He sits on high, at the right hand of His Eternal Father; but Bethlehem, with its wondrous scenes, is recalled to our minds, and whilst we give homage to Him in His humiliation, we implore grace and mercy for ourselves. You ask, "was it an Infant that taught the Saviour's doctrine, and worked mighty signs and wonders?" I answer it was He who lay an Infant in the arms of His Mother. In Him were "hidden all the treasures of the wisdom and knowledge of God." He was, even in His infantile state, the God of majesty, whom the angels adore with trembling. The self-same Son of the Eternal appeared a helpless babe, who redeemed us by His sufferings. What you say in regard to the image of the "Bambino Gesu," at Rome, is an instance of the piety of individuals, who at a critical moment ask for relief from our Lord through His holy Mother, whose happy parturition they specially honor. You call our devotion to the Blessed Virgin *Mariolatry;* yet you must perceive in the pious exercises at which you carp, enough to qualify their meaning. It may relieve you to be informed that as most of them are not sanctioned much less enjoined by authority, the most devoted Catholic may abstain from their use. Idolatry, you remark, consists in giving the attributes of God to creatures, and you allege that we ascribe omnipresence, omniscience, and omnipotence to Mary; but if you reflect that we recognize her as a mere creature, having no excellence or power of herself, you will perceive that she can have no divine attribute. God is essentially self-existent, independent, and sovereign. Mary is always addressed as a suppliant at his throne, which necessarily excludes all idea of divine power or perfection. You take exception at her being styled in some private devotion 'Temple of the Trinity;' but is not every Christian such in some degree? "Ye are the temple of the living God."* Omniscience implies boundless knowledge derived from no other. Our communion with the world of spirits is carried on with great simplicity. We learn from Scripture that the angels are present, and witnesses of our thoughts, and we conceive the Saints and their Queen to have the like knowledge, without troubling ourselves to understand the manner in which God imparts it to them.

You are pleased to review some of the texts of Scripture which regard the Blessed Virgin.

* 2 Cor. vi. 16.

The angelical salutation: "Hail, full of grace;" is translated in your Bible: "Hail, thou that art highly favored;" which you maintain is much more faithful to the Greek words. Bloomfield, the Protestant commentator, approves the Vulgate version, observing, after Valcknaer, that verbs of this form imply heaping up, or filling up. What is more important, the Syriac version, made in the first or second age, has precisely words corresponding to the Latin:—

ܫܠܡ ܠܟܝ ܡܠܝܬ ܛܝܒܘܬܐ

"Peace be to thee, full of goodness."

Whatever tyros, to whom you refer, may think, scholars will scarcely agree with you that our version, which is almost as ancient as the Syriac, is "an unwarrantable gloss upon the original." As Syriac was the language used by the angel, being the vernacular tongue, it must be supposed that the Syriac interpreter gave the precise terms, which were probably retained in the pious exercises of the faithful. You confess the force of the prophecy, uttered by the Virgin herself: "Behold, from henceforth, all generations shall call me blessed." "This," you say, "is undoubtedly high honor to the Virgin; but it is limited plainly to the estimation of the *saints below*." I see in it no such limitation. The saints in glory no doubt regard as blessed above all other creatures, Her who was chosen to be the living tabernacle of the Incarnate God. Those who have loved

Him most on earth, have always honored her with profound veneration. You "claim your full share in the honor due to her;" but how do you manifest it? Is it by your systematic endeavors to decry devotion to her as idolatry? Is it by seeking out matter of reproach to show her sinfulness?

You remark that our Saviour never calls her Mother, but woman. Is it not sufficient that the inspired evangelists frequently call her by that glorious name—"the mother of Jesus?" The inspired Elizabeth likewise styled her "the mother of my Lord." It was meet that our Lord Himself should abstain from it when He was called on to exercise His miraculous power, over which she had no control. Yet, as Bloomfield again remarks, "woman" was a term of affection and respect. If the words of our Lord, addressed to her when she sought a miraculous supply of wine, to relieve the parties from confusion at not being able to furnish their guests, imply independence of Her control in such works, as St. Augustin understands them, they do not certainly intimate a refusal. The fact explains itself. She immediately directed the waiters to look for His orders, which she felt confident would be given. Forthwith He bade them fill the vases with water, which, when brought to the master of the banquet, proved to be delicious wine. "He clearly shows," says St. Cyril of Alexandria, "how much parents should be honored, by proceeding at once to the performance of the miracle for His mother's sake, which otherwise He would have deferred."* It may please you better to hear the Protestant Archbishop Newcome: "When our Lord had given this gentle rebuke,—He suffered her request to sway Him, and seems to have made the first display of His glorious power partly in deference to her."

You dwell on the silence of the Scripture in regard to her piety and virtue, as if the fact of her having been chosen to be Mother of God were not sufficient to warrant the belief of her high excellence and perfection. The belief of the mystery of God Incarnate, which preceded the writing of the New Testament, was necessarily attended with high esteem of the holy One who was its chief and immediate instrument. But although no elaborate panegyric of her virtues was framed by the sacred penmen, an angel proclaimed her acceptance with God, and the fulness of grace with which she was adorned. Her faith is declared eminent by Elizabeth, because she believed the revelation made to her by the heavenly messenger. Several times it is stated, that she treasured up in her heart the things that regarded her Divine Child, and weighed them attentively. That she stood at the foot of the cross is more to her praise, than

* In *locum.*

if she had followed Him throughout His journeys, when thousands hung with admiration on His lips. It showed the tender, steadfast, fearless affection of a mother; it showed fortitude greater than that of woman. Her unassuming modesty, her meek devotion and profound humility, are sufficiently indicated by the silence of the sacred writers on other occasions, when it was a matter of honor and pleasure to be near Jesus. She is especially mentioned as being in the company of the Apostles, when the Holy Ghost, in tongues of fire, descended on them. It was not her province to interfere with the government of the Church, which was confided to them—it became her not to dictate; but she persevered with them in prayer, and can we doubt that her supplications gave increased force to theirs? Would you have hesitated to ask her to pray to her Divine Son for you, if you had lived at that time? Would you have thought your chance of success equal without her aid? She is now near Him in glory—her maternal relation being not dissolved, as you most strangely fancy, but confirmed and illustrated by higher gifts and prerogatives, than suited her state of pilgrimage. Saints and Angels, Cherubs and Seraphs must be amazed that a daughter of Eve should have been made worthy to give of her own substance the matter of which the Body of God's own Son was formed,—to bear Him as in a shrine,—to bring Him forth,—to see, to touch Him with the familiarity and fondness of a mother. His affection for her was natural, as well as holy; and as on earth He yielded to her requests, even when it seemed a departure from the ordinary rules of His high Providence, so in heaven He grants her, with filial kindness, the favors which she implores for frail mortals. All this you may regard as fond imagining; but it is founded in the natural, indissoluble tie which binds the mother to the Son—in the very mystery itself, in which Mary gave to the world our Redeemer, and was thus made the channel of communicating to us every grace and blessing. For this reason, St. Bernard says, "Let us cling to Mary, let us venerate her with all our heart, since such is the will of God, who decreed that we should have all through Mary."*

Instead of offering you my own reflections on those passages which seem to you to show, that "the Blessed Redeemer refused to attach any spiritual pre-eminence to the earthly relationship of His mother," I will lay before you the remarks of St. Ambrose, on Luke viii. 20: "He did not mean to reject the attentions of His mother; for He Himself commands, 'Let whosoever dishonors father or mother, die the death;' but He acknowledges Himself obliged to attend rather to the mysteries of His Father,

* Serm. in Nat. B. V. Mariæ.

than to indulge maternal affection. His mother is not disowned here (as some heretics insidiously pretend); even from the cross He acknowledges her." The words in parenthesis are not mine, but those of Ambrose. What you regard as an intimation, that the temporary relation of mother and Son was at an end,*—an absurdity, not to say an impiety,—St. Ambrose takes as a splendid proof of tender affection on the part of the expiring Saviour. He remarks, that John alone records what "the others passed over in silence,—how Christ on the cross addressed His mother, deeming it of greater importance to state, that He who triumphed over torments and punishments, the conqueror of the devil, performed the duties of filial affection, than that He bestowed the kingdom of heaven. For if it be an edifying fact, that pardon is given by the Lord to a robber, it is far more edifying that the mother is honored by her Son. But neither was Mary wanting in what became her as mother of Christ; since whilst the Apostles fled away, she stood before the cross, and with tearful eyes looked on the wounds of her Son; for she did not look to the death of her beloved, but to the salvation of the world."†

I am sorry to find you asserting that in the time of Augustin the Virgin Mary was not

* Vol. ii. p. 75.

† In Luc. l. x c. xiii.

called "the Mother of God," whilst St. Cyril of Alexandria proved to the fathers of Ephesus, in the council held the year after the death of Augustin, 431, that this title had always been given her, and was necessarily implied in the mystery of the Incarnation; which they also confirmed. What Augustin says, that "so far as concerned His Deity, He had no mother," is a self-evident truth; "but it is also true," as he adds, "that so far as concerned His humanity, He had." "For the Lord of heaven and earth came by a woman. He was made of a woman. He was the son of Mary." This is what the Catholic Church holds. You quote Augustin, as affirming that "Mary from Adam was dead, because of sin;" which words are the more common reading of a passage in his commentary on the thirty-fourth psalm. It is well for you to know that in the Vatican and Colbertine manuscripts the reading is different: "Mary from Adam, Adam died because of sin;" and then is added: "the flesh of the Lord, from Mary, died to cancel sins." The other passage which you object, says of our Redeemer: "His flesh ALONE was not the flesh of sin, because His mother conceived Him not by concupiscence, but by grace." This justly proves that He alone, in virtue of His supernatural conception, was exempt from sin. "All the flesh of others is the flesh of sin," because all others, in consequence of their natural conception, are subject to that sin which is common to all the posterity of fallen man. Whether Augustin meant thereby to deny any privilege or exemption, even in regard of her from whom the flesh of Christ was taken, I venture not to say; but he himself has warned us that in general expressions, however strong, he does not mean to include the Blessed Mother of our Lord. In arguing against the Pelagians, he stated that all men but Christ alone, even the eminent servants of God, are sinners, and fall into sin; and supposing some one to object the instances of several saints, whose virtues are praised in Scripture, and among them, the Virgin, he answers with confidence, that if they were to reappear on earth they would all acknowledge themselves to have been sinners, with the exception of her alone; "excepting, therefore, the Holy Virgin, of whom when treating of sins, I am altogether unwilling to entertain any question, for the honor of the Lord; for hence we know that greater grace was bestowed on her to overcome sin in every respect, as she was made worthy to conceive and bring forth Him who certainly was without sin."*

You surprise me, Right Reverend Sir, by the novel meaning which you assign to the term θεότοκος or *Deipara*, which you translate *Godbearer*. It certainly was employed by the Council of Ephesus to express "Mother of God." All reasoning against her maternity is destroyed by the

* L. de Natura et Gratia, c. xxxvi. n. 42.

Apostle, who says, that "God has sent His Son made of a woman."* Your views of this subject are utterly opposed to sound doctrine, as solemnly declared by that ancient Council, on the authority of the Sacred Scripture and of apostolic tradition. "To constitute *a mother*," you say, "the woman must produce a living creature which has *derived its nature and its qualities* through her instrumentality, so that it is of the *same race*, and is truly her *offspring* or *progeny*." According to this reasoning Mary was not the mother of Jesus! Did she not conceive Him, according to the prophecy of Isaiah, as well as bring Him forth? Do you imagine, with some of the followers of Apollinaris, that His flesh was not taken from her substance, by the Divine operation of the Holy Ghost, but gliding down from heaven, passed through her as a conduit? Every one who has a correct view of this mystery must be shocked at your language, which betrays the most erroneous views. Dr. Nevin has truly said: "The man cannot be right at heart in regard to the faith of the Incarnation, whose tongue falters in pronouncing Mary Mother of God!" This is the great source of opposition to the veneration of the Blessed Virgin. The mystery of the Incarnation is incorrectly viewed, and men who have but vague notions of it, from want of theological training,

* Gal. iv. 4.

are easily offended at the consequences which necessarily flow from it when rightly understood. The Church, on the contrary, by cherishing this devotion, leads her children to give constant homage to the mystery on which it is founded.

Allow me to draw your attention to other erroneous language which has escaped you, in your effort to depreciate the maternal rights of the Virgin. "That relationship is a question of the body. The heavenly relationship is a question of the soul." The body of Christ was, of course, formed of the substance of His mother, whilst His soul was created and united with it by the act of Divine Power; but the relationship of the Son to the Father is the relationship of the Second Divine Person to the First Divine Person, which subsisted from eternity. The assumption of the human nature, body and soul, by the second Divine Person, constitutes the mystery of the Incarnation. If you refer to this relationship, it is by no means confined to the soul, since the Apostle expressly says: "Thou hast fitted me a body;" intimating thereby, that Christ in the flesh offered the atonement. The God man, therefore, is the Son of God, the Father; the second Divine Person having assumed, not the body alone but the human nature. He is also the Son of Mary, the body united with His soul being assumed by Him. Mary is the Mother not of the mere flesh of Christ, but of Christ Himself, as our parents are called such, although our souls be created by the direct action of God. For this reason she is called, and is Mother of God, an appellation so closely connected with the mystery, that it was made, as Dr. Nevin well observes, a *tessera*, or standard of orthodoxy, by the Council of Ephesus, no less strictly than the term consubstantial had been made such by the Nicene fathers. To suppose that the Divine Person supplied the place of the soul, is the heresy of Apollinaris, condemned in the fifth century; to deny that Mary is Mother of God, is to renew the exploded heresy of Nestorius.

The corporal assumption of the Blessed Virgin into heaven, although not an article of Catholic faith, is an ancient tradition, of which you find traces in St. Epiphanius. The narrative given by St. John of Damascus has been inserted in the Breviary; but you are aware that this does not put it beyond question. The celebration of the feast by the Church affords the strongest argument in support of the fact, although, as the object of it is not specially defined, we can suspend our assent, without derogating from her authority, or incurring censure. You are mistaken in conceiving that the Virgin is thus put on a level with her Son, whose ascension is believed on the testimony of the Sacred Scriptures. There is an obvious difference between the terms assumption and ascension, the former term implying the act of Almighty God, who takes to happiness His humble handmaid—

the latter designating the act of Christ Himself, who by His own divine power, rose to the highest heavens. You may not feel satisfied with the evidence of the ancient tradition; but it is remarkable that it should at all exist, if without foundation, since the early Christians were wont to preserve the remains of the eminent servants of God; and yet none ever boasted that they possessed the body of the Virgin.

St. Basil interprets the prophecy of Simeon, that a sword should pierce the Virgin's soul, of some fluctuation or agitation of mind, *σαλεύμος*, when beholding the crucifixion; but for which he seems to think she would not have needed the application of His Blood. This regards perplexity of mind, rather than moral fault; yet even so you will scarcely insist upon its correctness. The sublime prediction marked the agonies of her maternal heart, as she stood at the foot of the cross; which did not imply any defect on her part. The narrative of the Evangelist gives no indication of it, but presents her as a model of fortitude, as well as of maternal affection, standing, where other mothers would have swooned away. You know, Right Reverend Sir, that our respect for the authority of the fathers does not oblige us to accept the interpretations which individuals among them may give of particular passages of Scripture.

The testimony of Popes Leo and Gregory establish the stainless perfection of our Redeemer as necessarily resulting from His supernatural conception, and the assumption of the human nature by the second Divine Person. Such general expressions can scarcely avail to exclude a privilege such as the Church recognizes in the Virgin, especially since the same writers elsewhere express the most exalted sentiments of her dignity. St. Gregory, in his commentary on the books of Kings, speaks of her as one "who transcended, by the dignity to which she was chosen, the highest elect creatures;" and as a mystical mountain, whose height is above that of all others. "Is not Mary a high mountain, since in order to be worthy to conceive the Eternal Word, the summit of her merits rose above all the choirs of angels, even to the throne of the Deity?"*

St. Epiphanius justly condemned the superstition of the Collyridians, who had priestesses offering cakes to the Virgin, whence they derived their name. He forbade all worship to be given her, such as is given to God, but he encouraged all to honor her, as the Mother of our Lord. The ambiguity of the term "worship," by which you render the Greek, enables you to use his testimony with effect for such as take words in their popular signification, without regard to the circumstances in which they are employed.†

It is injurious to our Lord Himself, as well as to His Virgin Mother and St. Joseph, to suppose,

* L. i. in 1 Reg. c. i. n. 5. † L. iii. p. 400, E.

with you, that when they missed Him, as they were about to return from Jerusalem, they sought Him amongst their kinsfolk and acquaintance, "as if he were a common youth, seeking to amuse Himself during the religious festival." Such a thought could not have entered into their minds. They supposed Him to be on His way home in the company of their kinsfolk, and sought Him accordingly in the different bands of travellers, His age allowing Him to go with either company of men or women. They knew well that He was fully intent on doing the will of His Father, but they were not aware that He would have manifested His wisdom in the temple at that early period of His life. Accordingly, after a day's journey, being convinced that He had remained behind for some high purpose, they returned. His Mother ventured to inquire of Him the reason of His leaving them in anxiety and pain. His answer shows, indeed, that His first care was to fulfil the will of His Heavenly Father, but it does not imply any disregard of her maternal claims on His affection and obedience. The fact that "He went down with them, and was subject to them,"* puts this beyond contradiction.

It is somewhat extraordinary, that after such a determined effort to depreciate the dignity and merits of the Holy Mother of our Lord, you

* Luke ii. 51.

should have ventured to quote the passages of the ancient Liturgies, especially those in use at Jerusalem, Constantinople, and Alexandria, which so highly extol her. They contain those expressions of her Divine maternity, which, to you, appear so low and sensuous, although they are sanctioned by Holy Writ, which tells us that St. Elizabeth, inspired by the Holy Ghost, pronounced blessed the fruit of her womb. Your delicacy shrinks from such plain language. The Liturgy, bearing the name of St. James, was used at Jerusalem before the days of St. Cyril, whose fifth catechesis makes evident reference to it. In this the Virgin is styled: "Our most Holy, immaculate, superlatively blessed, and glorious Lady, the Mother of God, and ever Virgin Mary." The singers assisting at the Holy Sacrifice say: "It is meet that we should magnify thee, the ever blessed, immaculate parent and mother of God, who art of more honor than the cherubim, and incomparably more glorious than the seraphim." Again they sing: "Thou, O full of grace, art the joy of the whole creation, both of angels and men; a temple of holiness; a spiritual paradise, and the glory of virginity, of whom the Deity was incarnate, and our God, whose being was from eternity, was made a child. For thy womb was His throne, the seat of Him whom the heavens cannot contain."* Do you find in our devotional

* Vol. ii. p. 86.

books anything more sublime in praise of the Virgin Mother? This language is common to all the ancient liturgies, and is still employed by the Greeks, who style the Virgin "all holy, stainless, superlatively blessed, and glorious Lady, the Mother of God, and ever Virgin Mary." It is generally admitted by the learned, that the liturgies, in their actual form, can be traced back to the fifth century, and that they contain the substance of worship as prescribed by the Apostles, so that wherever there is a general agreement in their language, it affords the strongest presumption of apostolic tradition. Here you find this entire harmony, which you would fain disturb by conjecturing that these liturgies have been interpolated in this regard. You do not indeed venture openly to dispute their authority, but you observe that they contain prayers for the Virgin and the saints. A closer inspection may convince you, that they are commemorated, only as Abraham and David are mentioned in various parts of Scripture, to lay before God their merits and services, that through regard for them, He may have mercy on us; and to show the communion which unites the saints already glorified with the faithful on earth. In fact, you yourself give passages from the liturgies of St. Chrysostom and St. Basil, in which Christ is implored to pardon sin "through the intercessions of His ever spotless and Virgin Mother;" and again of her and all the saints: "for the sake of whose prayers and intercessions, have mercy upon us." In the Ethiopian liturgy we read: "May all their prayers for us be accepted." St. Cyril closes his commemoration in like manner: "That God, through their prayers and supplications, may receive our prayers."* But you observe that no address to Mary, or the saints, in the form of prayer, is contained in these liturgies. The same remark may be made in regard to the Roman Missal, at this day. The more ancient and solemn mode of intercessory prayer is the indirect one; but it is the same in substance as the more popular mode of addressing the saints themselves. In imitation of the Scripture style: "Remember Thy servant David, O Lord, and all his meekness;" the priest begs of God to remember His departed servants, and for their sakes to grant us mercy. All those objections which you urge against Dr. Milner's theory of a revelation being made by God to the saints, may be here again urged; but the fact of this form having come down from the apostolic times, shows satisfactorily that they are groundless. Besides, the difficulty which you advance, of the prayer being heard, may also be alleged against the praise which is here devoutly given to the Mother of God; and must be as easy of solution in both cases. All that you allege against any mediation but that of Christ, our Redeemer, is equally applicable to this ancient

* Vol. ii. p. 86.

usage, as to our direct addresses, so that we stand or fall with the Basils and Chrysostoms, and the churches of Jerusalem, Antioch, and Alexandria. If you admit these formularies, you cannot consistently censure our practice.

Dr. Milner referred to St. Irenæus, who calls Mary the advocate of Eve, having compensated by her obedience for the disobedience of our first mother. You avow the difficulty of explaining this text, but deny that it can have reference to prayers offered by Mary for Eve, who was dead more than four thousand years, or that it can authorize us to seek her prayers. The meaning of the saint is not quite so incomprehensible. He draws a parallel between our frail parent and the Virgin Mother of our Lord: "As Eve was seduced through the speech of an angel, that she might depart from God, and violate His word; so Mary, through the speech of an angel, was evangelized so as to bear God, being obedient to His word. And if Eve disobeyed God, yet Mary was persuaded to obey God, that the Virgin Mary might become the advocate of the virgin Eve. And as the human race was bound to death through a virgin, it is saved through a virgin; the scales being equally balanced;—virginal disobedience by virginal obedience."* You perceive, Right Reverend Sir, the prominent part which this early father, after St. Justin, ascribes to Mary in the great work of redemption. The fate of Eve was

* Adv. hær. l. v. c. xix.

sealed four thousand years before; but it was only in anticipation of the atonement to be offered on Calvary, by the Son of Mary, that her offence was pardoned. The obedience of Mary to the angel's message was present to the Divine Mind, with the mystery to be accomplished on her assent, and thus she became virtually an intercessor for her frail mother. If then her advocacy thus anticipated availed Eve, so we may hope that it will prove profitable to those who now earnestly seek it.

The contrast which you form between our professions of devotion and confidence towards God and our Saviour Jesus Christ, and those which we use to the Blessed Virgin, is wholly without foundation; for as we acknowledge her to be a mere creature, and to possess no gift or power, unless by the free concession of the Creator, on account of her intimate relation to Christ, there is an essential difference in the force of all our expressions and acts regarding her. God is an independent, all-sufficient, eternal Being. Jesus Christ, the God-man, has, as God, all the divine attributes in their fulness; and His human nature is replenished with all holiness, in virtue of its assumption by the second Divine Person. "No other name under heaven is given to men, whereby they can be saved." These principles being fixed and unchangeable, the devotional expressions employed towards the Virgin are necessarily qualified, and must be interpreted without prejudice to the Divine perfections, or to the essential mediatorship of Christ. If you understood this matter practically, you would soon feel that all is harmony, where you fancy rivalry and opposition. We flee to Mary, as to the Mother of our Redeemer, asking her to plead with her Divine Son, and obtain through His Blood pardon of our manifold offences. You are offended that she should be styled Queen of Heaven, which implies only that she is first and greatest of the saints. But what place would you assign her? It is her peculiar privilege to be the Mother of our Divine Redeemer; and must she not be nearest to Him in glory?

LETTER XIII.

On the Veneration of the Saints.

RIGHT REVEREND SIR:

THE honor which we render to the saints and angels, and the petitions which we address to them, that they may intercede with God for us, are censured by you as idolatrous. In order to support this charge, you avail yourself of an equivocal term employed by the great controvertist Bellarmin, when explaining the manner in which vows are made to the saints. He maintains that vows, strictly so called, imply a solemn promise to God; and adds that vows made to the saints, are made to them only inasmuch as they partake of His glory, being united with Him. In this sense he uses the terms, "*dii per participationem.*"* Instead of cavilling at a word so carefully qualified, you should have reflected, as you elsewhere admit, that "it is not the giving the name of God to a creature which constitutes the sin of idolatry."† This term, without the accompanying limitation, is applied by the sacred penman to the judges, as acting under divine authority.‡ In order to

* De Eccl. Triumph. l. iii. c. ix.

† Vol. ii. p. 63.

‡ Ps. lxxxi. 6; John x. 34.

give coloring to your censure, you translate the term *divus*, God, when applied to the saints, although you must know that in our usage it bears no such meaning. This may gratify the bigot, or mislead the unlearned: it cannot supply the place of argument.

We reverence the saints only as servants of God, on whom He bestowed the gifts of His grace, and the glory of His kingdom. We acknowledge in them no perfection which is not derived from His bounty; and we ascribe to them no power, independent of His free concession. Through the merits of Christ our Saviour, they have been sanctified and rendered triumphant over the enemy of souls, and through His atonement must be obtained whatever we hope from their prayers in our behalf. We give them not that glory which belongs to God, for we know that He is jealous of His honor; but we honor them for His sake, and to Him we refer ultimately all homage, saying with the Apostle: "To the King of ages, immortal and invisible, the only God, be honor and glory."* With our whole heart we say with the holy deacon, whose words you recite from St. Augustin, that we do not adore, but honor them. The term worship, which you employ, is ambiguous.

As you are unprepared to admit that the early Christians gave religious veneration to the good

* 1 Tim. i. 17.

angels, you translate the celebrated passage of St. Justin after this manner: "We worship and adore Him and His Son who came out from Him (and hath taught us respecting these things, and respecting the host of the other good angels who follow Him, and are made like unto Him), and the Prophetic Spirit, honoring them in reason and in truth."* I take leave to submit the translation given in the collection called "The Faith of Catholics," which is strictly literal, beginning somewhat higher to give a clearer view: "Hence we have also been called Atheists, and we confess that we are unbelievers (*Atheists*) of such pretended gods, but not of the most true (*God*) and Father of righteousness and temperance, and of the other virtues, and of a God in whom there is no mixture of evil; but both Him, and the Son who came from Him, and taught us those things, and the host of the other good angels that follow and resemble (*Him, or them*), and the Prophetic Spirit, we venerate and adore, honoring in reason and truth, and freely delivering, to every one who wishes to learn, even as we have been taught."† To those who understand the structure of a Greek sentence, it will not appear possible to admit your parenthesis, with the insertion of the

* Vol. ii. p. 99.

† Αλλ' ἐκεῖνον τὲ, καὶ τὸν παρ' αὐτȣ̃ ὑιὸν ἐλθοντα καὶ διδαξαντα ἡμᾶς ταῦτα καὶ τὸν τῶν ἄλλων ἑπομενων καὶ ἐξομοιȣμένων ἀγαθων ἀγγέλων στρατὸν, πνεῦμα τὲ το προφητικὸν σεβομεθα καὶ προσκυνȣμεν. Apol. I. n. 6.

term "respecting;" but as this may be too abstruse a discussion for most readers, I will content myself with giving the passage in the note, and leave you to justify your translation to the learned. It may embarrass some to hear St. Justin speak of venerating and adoring, if the preceding terms regard the angels as the objects of veneration, but as they chiefly regard God the Father, and His Son, on whom the angels are represented as waiting in attendance, and to whom they are said to bear resemblance, the terms must chiefly be applied to the Divine Persons, and to the angels only in their relation to them. In addressing Pagans, for whom the apology was intended, it was unnecessary to make nice distinctions, especially as the terms were then applied without much discrimination, to various acts of religious worship. The other passages of St. Justin, which you quote, throw no new light on this text. He elsewhere says, that Christians adored the Creator, the Son, who taught us the truths of life, and the Prophetic Spirit,* without mentioning the good angels in connection with the Son, which is not surprising, since it was unnecessary to repeat that which was only secondary and subordinate in worship. Again, he observes that Christians pay tribute, giving to Cæsar the things which are of Cæsar, to God the things which are of God; and in this connection he observes: "We therefore adore

* Ibidem, n. 13.

God alone, but cheerfully serve you in other matters."* This worship of God alone is of course that supreme honor which to Him alone is due, and which the Gentiles wished to be given to idols. It nowise excludes that veneration of the good angels, in honoring whom they honored the followers of God's only Son.

You quote Dr. Milner's answer to the objection that the invocation of the saints involves, of necessity, a belief in their omnipresence: "How does it follow, from my praying to an angel or a saint, in any place, that I *necessarily believe the angel or saint to be in that place?* Was Elisha really in Syria when he saw the ambush prepared there for the King of Israel?—(2 Kings, vi. 9.) BUT IT IS SUFFICIENT THAT GOD IS ABLE TO REVEAL TO THEM THE PRAYERS OF CHRISTIANS WHO ADDRESS THEM HERE ON EARTH."† You do not, as far as I can perceive, explain the fact, or meet the reasoning; but, as if the Divine revelation here spoken of implied on the part of God a formal communication to the saints of the prayers addressed to them, you ridicule the idea, and amuse your readers with some curious calculations of the number of *Ave Marias* daily recited. This low view of a supernatural operation is justly rejected by the author of Tract No. 71. "When it is said that the saints cannot hear our prayers, unless God reveal them to them; so that Almighty God, upon

* Ibidem, n. 17.

† Vol. II. p. 43.

the Roman theory, conveys from us to them those requests which they are to ask back again of Him for us, we are certainly using an unreal, because an unscriptural argument, Moses, on the Mount, having the sin of his people first revealed to him by God, that he in turn might intercede with God for them. Indeed, it is through Him, in whom we live, and move, and have our being, that we are able in *this* life to hear the requests of each other, and to present them to Him in prayer. Such an argument, then, while shocking and profane to the feelings of a Romanist, is shallow even in the judgment of a philosopher." Your illustrations, borrowed from the court of an earthly king, are sadly deficient. The revelation which God made to His prophets of things distant, or future, was a communication of Divine light, in which these were presented; and His revelation to His glorified saints, as conceived by St. Thomas Aquinas, is a manifestation by which they view, as in a mirror, all that it concerns them to know. In these days, when information is communicated with the speed of lightning to parts the most distant, shall men continue to measure the knowledge of spirits by natural rules, and prescribe limits beyond which it cannot extend? Most people ascribe to the devil greater knowledge than you are willing to admit in the saints.

By some chance you pass over the chief points on which Dr. Milner insists, and leave a great *hiatus* in your quotation, without giving any hint of it to your readers. After the passage from 2 Kings, vi. 9, he proceeds: "Again, we know that there is joy before the angels of God over one sinner that repenteth. (Luke xv. 10.) Now is it by visual rays, or undulating sounds, that these blessed spirits in heaven know what passes in the hearts of men upon earth? How does his Lordship (*the Bishop of Durham*) know, that one part of the saint's felicity may not consist in contemplating the wonderful ways of God's providence, with all His creatures here on earth?" This might have been worthy of some notice, but it was more convenient to pass it over.

May I add, that it appears to me sufficient that the saints know in general the usage of asking their intercession, without any special knowledge of the petitions addressed to them. They may plead with God for all who desire their prayers, and thus benefit them in proportion to the earnestness with which each one supplicates them. I do not, however, doubt that they have a clear intuition of the prayers themselves, in the Divine light with which they are replenished. You, yourself, admit that they plead with God for men, and you even suppose them to be acquainted with the commemoration made of them in the Liturgy. Concerning the faithful, you ask: "Do they not desire that *he* (*the departed saint*) *may remember them*, when he joins the blessed spirits of the just made perfect.

Do they not hope that the privilege of his prayers to God, on their behalf, may still be continued to them, now that he is removed so much nearer to the Fountain of all grace and heavenly benediction?"* You thus admit their intercession, and their knowledge of the commemoration made of them on earth. You explain the testimony of St. Chrysostom regarding the refreshment and joy which departed souls derive from prayer offered in the sacrifice, of the satisfaction which is afforded them by knowing that they are still loved and remembered by the faithful on earth!

You are scandalized, Right Reverend Sir, at various expressions in the Litany of St. Joseph, who, among many very high-sounding titles, is styled "Ruler of the Lord of the Universe." These were used to express that subjection which our Lord practised to Joseph, as well as to Mary, as Luke testifies. But it may relieve you to be informed that Litanies are not in favor with the authorities at Rome, excepting the few very ancient and general formularies, found in the Breviaries, Missals, Pontificals, and Rituals, with the Litany of Loretto. The Rules of the Index forbid them all, although the Litany of Jesus has subsequently been sanctioned. I trust, that in this respect at least, they will meet your cordial approval. If you ask me,

* Vol. ii. p. 305.

why they appear in our Prayer-Books, I must answer that this form of prayer is so popular, that our publishers despair of selling books which have not a good supply of Litanies, and the Bishops can scarcely urge the rule, without exciting grave murmurs. The terms employed, although sometimes bordering on exaggeration, are generally reducible to strict theological accuracy, and whilst they startle the indevout and unbelieving, express the outpourings of a heart earnest in its appeals for mercy, through its favorite advocate.

You deny that "there is any power in the Church militant to decide what individuals the Lord may have chosen to glorify"* among His saints; but do you question the propriety of honoring the memory of the Apostles? Do you blame the early Christians, who met on the anniversary of illustrious martyrs, such as Ignatius and Polycarp, and gave God thanks, in solemn worship, for their triumph? It was thus, as you know, that the practice of celebrating the festivals of the saints was introduced. The process of canonization is a safeguard against mistake, which supposes miraculous evidence of the acceptance of the individual with God. Such evidence being furnished, it is God who manifests His good pleasure to glorify His servant. The edification afforded to the faithful by the

* Ib. p. 96.

public judgment and testimony of the chief Bishop, founded on it, is a sufficient reason for proposing the virtues of the saint to veneration, since we are more easily influenced by example than by precept. If St. Paul ventured to propose himself as a model to others, inasmuch as he studied to imitate Christ, it cannot be unbecoming for the Pope to propose to the Church at large the examples of men, who have been found true followers of our Lord. St. Francis de Sales, St. Charles Borromeo, and others, exercise a happy influence in the cause of virtue, far greater than they could have exercised had not the Church proclaimed their sanctity and happiness.

The infidel Gibbon ascribed to the honors given by the early Christians to the martyrs, the ardor with which so many exposed themselves to death for the faith, and the great increase of Christians.

Your reasoning on the miracles ascribed to the saints, is not very philosophical. Those recorded in Scripture are, indeed, supported by all those evidences which prove Christianity, and are consequently far more credible than facts which are unconnected with a great moral revolution. Yet miracles, accompanied with the conversion of a nation, such as those of Augustin in England, Xavier in the Indies and Japan, derive great credibility from an event so extraordinary. The miracles recorded in every age of the Church, by witnesses of great integrity and discernment, are not easily to be discarded, although we should be slow to believe any deviation from the ordinary course of things without strong proof. Facts attested by witnesses above suspicion, and approved by a tribunal remarkable for its severe scrutiny, should not be slightly rejected. In making light of evidence supporting modern miracles, a disposition may be fostered adverse to the belief of the Gospel miracles themselves, and men may be tempted to view with distrust, if not to mock, all that is supernatural. Your language is far from being characterized by that moderation which your very solemn professions might lead us to expect. "True, indeed, it is, that the impiety of your Popes has presumed to institute the old heathen *apotheosis*, by enrolling some hundreds of saints amongst the angelic hosts, and authorizing your deluded people to address their prayers to them, as the ancient pagans did to their *Dii minorum gentium.*"* You, sir, are the fit person to speak of "the atrocious malignity of spirit" of Dr. Milner.† You are mistaken in ascribing the ridicule of Voltaire and Rousseau to "the false miracles of Popery, connected with the notorious licentiousness of the priesthood," for their satire was chiefly directed against the Holy Scriptures, and they paid, from

* P. 379. † P. 381.

time to time, homage to the virtues of our religious communities. Voltaire avows, that "it is undeniable that eminent virtues have adorned the cloister. Scarcely any monastery is without admirable souls, who do honor to human nature. Too many writers have taken delight in seeking out the disorders and vices by which these asylums of piety were sometimes defiled. It is certain that the life of seculars has been always more vicious, and that the greatest crimes have not been committed in monasteries; but their vices have been more remarked from their contrast with the Rule."*

* Essai sur l'Histoire, t. iv. ch. cxxxv.

LETTER XIV.

On Relics.

RIGHT REVEREND SIR:

YOUR answer to Dr. Milner's argument in favor of the veneration of relics, is by no means satisfactory. His statement of the mind of the Church is fully sustained by the Council of Trent, which you yourself cite, and by the second Council of Nice, which you have misunderstood. The object of the Nicene fathers was to vindicate the Church from the charge of superstition and idolatry in the reverence paid by her to the memorials of the saints, and they very properly referred to the usages prevailing among themselves, by which this veneration was testified. Their anathemas do not fall on such as omit these practices, which are devotional; but only on those who condemn them, and ground on them their unwarrantable charges. The assertion of Dr. Milner, that such usages are no essential part of religion, is perfectly consistent with the canon of this Council, cited by you, which requires relics to be deposited on the altars; because, though this be not essential, yet the Church is at liberty to enjoin that which is pious, and calculated to bring to the minds of the faithful the martyrs, who are represented in the Apocalypse as under the altar on which the Lamb stands as it were slain. The resuscitation of the dead man, when his corpse touched the bones of the prophet,* is an evidence that God sometimes manifests His favor towards His servants after their death, by miraculous operations; and it naturally suggests that their remains should be viewed with marked reverence. The preservation of the rod of Aaron, and of the vase containing manna, near the tabernacle, was a memorial of miraculous events, and bore a resemblance to the care which we employ in preserving sacred memorials with honor. The breaking in pieces of the brazen serpent, which had become an occasion of idolatry, shows that in case of abuse, the objects of religious veneration should be removed; but it proves nothing against due reverence being paid to them. The use of incense is an act of idolatry, when it is directed to supreme worship, as was the case with the heathen; but of itself it does not imply it, so that it depends on the intention, as also on external circumstances.

You refer to the burial of St. Stephen. Have you read in St. Augustin, Orosius, and other

* 4 Kings xiii. 21.

authors of the fifth century, the account of the divine revelation made of his relics, and of their being transported to Africa, carried in procession from place to place, and proving the instrument of many miracles? If you refuse to believe these venerable witnesses, I care not; but I remind you that they bear the most unequivocal testimony to the usage of venerating relics; and that they cannot be forced to your side, although you have ventured to quote a passage of St. Augustin which points out some abuses, altogether foreign to this holy practice. He states distinctly the fact: "They carry indeed the relics of the most blessed and glorious martyr Stephen, which your Holiness (he writes to the Bishop Quintilian) well knows how you should suitably honor, as we have done."* Again he says: "A little dust has gathered together so vast a multitude. The ashes are concealed; the favors are manifest. Reflect, dearly beloved, how great blessings God reserves for us in the land of the living, since He grants us such, by means of the dust of those who are departed."† You venture to quote St. Ambrose; but have you not read that he discovered, at Milan, the bodies of the martyrs Gervase and Protase, and testified with Augustin,‡ to miracles wrought on that occasion, appealing at the

* Ep. ccxii. alias ciii. ad Quintil.

† Serm. cccxvii. alias xcii. de diversis.

‡ L. xxii. de civ. Dei, c. viii.

same time to all the inhabitants of Milan, as knowing the facts? If Dr. Milner thus sported with authorities, you would have reason to say, that "he presumed greatly on the ignorance of his readers." In the work styled "The Church of the Fathers," written by Dr. Newman long before he became a Catholic, you will find full evidence of this ancient and pious usage. It is impossible to open the writings of the fathers of the fourth and fifth centuries, Gregory of Nazianzen, Basil, Chrysostom, or any other, without meeting, almost on every page, passages which prove that the remains of the martyrs were believed by all to be frequently the instruments of miraculous operations.

The tales about the relics of St. Thomas à Becket, are of no consequence whatever, where a principle is in question. His truly was a hallowed shrine, consecrated to the memory of a prelate who resisted the encroachments of the second Henry on the rights and privileges of the Church. The piety of the faithful had enriched it with costly ornaments, which excited the rapacity of Henry VIII., disturbed as he was by the silent reproach of the martyr. He accordingly abolished his festival, caused a mock trial to be held, and sentence to be passed on him as a traitor. His bones were to be exhumed, and publicly burnt; the plates of gold which covered his shrine were carried away, the gems with which it was studded were seized, one of them, of special lustre, the gift of Louis the Seventh, being thenceforward worn by the tyrant. These disgraceful proceedings might call even for your reprobation. As to relics which are not recommended by satisfactory testimony, Catholics are free to reject them. Let credulity be shunned; but let not a usage as ancient as the Church herself be wantonly condemned. Offerings made at shrines are usually silver tablets commemorative of some favor believed to have been obtained; not gifts to the priests. There is no rivalry between the saints and Christ their Lord. Every act done in their honor is grounded on the relation which they bear to Him, and redounds necessarily to His glory. You ask: "Did not our Lord know the humble faith of the woman who touched His garment, and *will* her recovery?" Certainly; but it was on the occasion of her performing that act with confidence in His power and goodness. No one expects any benefit from touching sacred memorials, unless in proportion to his faith, and to the benign will of the Almighty. "Did not St. Paul's prayers attend the use of those aprons and handkerchiefs?" This I know not. God may have granted the cures to show His approval of His servant and messenger, without any prayer specially directed by the Apostle to that end. But no matter. No one hopes for any Divine favor from the touch of any relic, unless through the prayers of the saint. You say that the garment of our Lord, and the aprons of St. Paul, were not relics, since their owners were then living on earth; but the principle is the same, since these material objects were made the instruments of miraculous cures on account of the relation they bore to Christ and to His apostle: and so the various objects which we call relics,—the bones of the saints, or things belonging to them, may be made the instruments of supernatural favors, when it so pleases God. That they have been such, is attested by all the illustrious writers of the fourth and fifth ages especially.

You observe: "No man of common feeling, or reflection, ever censured the wish even to preserve a relic of remarkable men or deeds, as an object of association, which must interest posterity."* In fact, an old box, which served Washington in the war of Independence, is preserved respectfully in the capitol; and the sword of the hero of New Orleans, has lately been presented with great formality to Congress. The feeling is natural and just, which leads us to cherish memorials of men whom we esteemed and loved. It is hallowed and ennobled by religion, and awakens a deeper sentiment and stronger affection. "But if you say to me," observes St. Ambrose, "what do you honor in that flesh which is already wasted and con-

* Ep. II. ad sororem Marcellin.

sumed? I honor in the flesh of the martyr the wounds which he received for the name of Christ; I honor the memory of one who still lives on account of his undying virtue; I honor ashes that have been consecrated by the confession of the Lord; I honor in those ashes the seeds of eternity; I honor the body which points out to me that I should love the Lord, and teaches me not to fear death for His sake. Why should not the faithful honor that body which even demons reverence? which indeed they afflicted in martyrdom, but which they glorify in the tomb? I honor, then, the body which Christ honored by the sword, and which will reign with Christ in heaven."*

If you compare this language, and that of the ancient fathers generally, with the language of the Breviary, or of Catholic preachers at this day, you will find no reason to accuse us of exaggerated views of the honor due to relics. The parallel which you draw between the heathenish superstitions which St. Cyril of Jerusalem describes, and the pious practices of devout Catholics, who humbly hope to be cured of infirmities through the intercession of the saints, has no foundation, since he expressly treats of the shrines of demons, or of their worship by superstitious rites performed near rivers. The confidence of the faithful in the early ages of the

* Serm. xciii. de S. Nazar. et Celso, in fine.

Church was equally as strong, nay, far stronger, because the instances of relief were frequent and striking.

What you give as a proof of superstition will not appear such even to your Protestant readers, when they understand the circumstances, namely, that the body of St. Isidore of Seville, was purchased at a great price, by Ferdinand I. King of Castile and Leon. Some might imagine that it was a matter of bargain and sale between Catholics; but the simple fact is, that the Saracens had possession of the country where his body was interred, and the Catholic king ransomed it at a large price, through veneration for his memory. The temple erected afterwards, in which it was deposited, was, of course, consecrated to Almighty God, to whom alone we dedicate all our churches, although, as it was designed to honor the memory of the holy Bishop of Seville, it bore his name, as is usual. The various miracles ascribed to his body, and those of other saints, do not surpass, if they equal, that which the Scripture relates of the bones of the prophet, the contact with which resuscitated a dead man; and cannot be rejected merely on account of their extraordinary character. Their credibility must be judged of by the rules of evidence.

The custom of kneeling to sovereigns, and the English usage of bowing before the vacant throne, are referred to by Dr. Milner, to vindicate the inferior and relative honor which we pay to sacred memorials. You, Right Reverend Sir, deemed it an honor to be allowed to bend the knee, and kiss the hand of Queen Victoria. Did you abjure your fidelity to God?

Assuredly every one understands that these very solemn marks of respect imply nothing incompatible with the Divine honor. You say: "Were nothing more than this involved in the doctrine or practice of Rome, we should never have thought the question worth an argument." Something more is implied in it, because the respect shown to princes is of a civil character, whilst that shown to sacred objects is religious; but both are inferior and subordinate, so that they are altogether different from the homage rendered to God. You speak of the worship of images and relics as profitable to the priests, thus endeavoring to prejudice your readers against our practice as interested: but I am an utter stranger to any pecuniary gain attached to it. I have visited the shrines of the saints, and bent before their images, and seen thousands perform the like acts of devotion, but I have never seen or known the smallest sum of money to be given or received on such an occasion. You may jeeringly speak of "the deluded multitude paying their offerings of silver and gold, to touch the holy coat at Treves, to adore the holy tooth of St. Peter, or to fall down before the winking statue of the Virgin of Ancona." I know nothing of St. Peter's tooth, and I have not visited Treves or Ancona, yet from the universal practice of all the countries in which I have travelled, or lived, I am perfectly assured that nothing whatever is demanded or given for any exhibition of relics. It is only in places like Westminster Abbey, which have passed into the hands of the stranger, that money is exacted for visiting the shrines and tombs of the saints.

The kissing of the Gospels in courts of justice, when an oath is taken, was alleged by Dr. Milner as an instance of religious honor rendered to a material object in reference to Christ our Lord, whose words they contain. This is perfectly analogous to our veneration of sacred memorials; yet you deny its force, because it is not alike in all the accompanying circumstances. "Where is the incense? where are the lights? where are the prayers of faith? where is the hope of receiving important aids and blessings? where is the association of the act with the alleged cures, the miraculous deliverance from sickness, calamity, and danger?" It is not necessary that all things should be alike, if the main point be the same. The act is plainly an expression of religious homage, the same which is performed by the priest when he kisses the Gospel at the altar. The incense and lights accompany it in the solemn celebration of the mysteries, both being directed in like manner to honor Christ, whose words are read to shed light on Jews and Gentiles. The effects hoped for occasionally from the application of sacred things are wholly distinct from the usage itself. It is rarely that they are sought, whilst the marks of religious honor are incessantly given to the precious memorials. That God has sometimes granted them is beyond all reasonable question. The cure of the afflicted woman by the touch of our Saviour's garment, and of many sick persons by the application of the handkerchiefs of St. Paul, prepare us for similar manifestations of Divine power in behalf of those, who, with faith and humility, seek relief in affliction.

Although it is notorious that St. Jerom defended the veneration of relics against Vigilantius, you have the courage to quote in your behalf, a passage selected from a letter written expressly for this purpose. That you may get due praise for your skill in drilling witnesses, I shall first state that the letter is addressed to the priest Riparius, who had informed St. Jerom of the attack, made somewhat in your own style, by Vigilantius on Catholics as "gatherers of ashes, and idolators, who venerated the bones of dead men." In reply, Jerom says: "We do not worship and adore, I do not say the relics of the martyrs, but not even the sun and moon, not the angels, not the archangels, not the cherubim, not the seraphim, or any name which is named either in this world or in the other, lest we should serve the creature, rather than the Creator, who is blessed forever." This is the passage which you quote. Now let your witness proceed with his testimony: "But we honor the relics of the martyrs, so as to adore Him whose martyrs they are. We honor the servants, that the honor may redound to the Lord, who says: 'He that receiveth you, receiveth Me.' Are then the relics of Peter and of Paul unclean? Is the body of Moses unclean, which, according to the Hebrew truth, was buried by the Lord Himself? and as often as we enter the basilics of the apostles and prophets, and of all the martyrs, do we venerate temples of idols? and are the lights which are lighted at their tombs, the evidences of idolatry?"* Now, sir, we will let the witness leave the stand.

* Ep. liii. ad Riparium.

LETTER XV.

On Sacred Images.

Right Reverend Sir:

I AM pleased to find that sacred images are unobjectionable in your eyes, as mere representations. "No sensible man," you say, "ever found fault with sculpture or painting as a memorial of past events, or of departed friends, or as a tribute to peculiar greatness, either in Church or State."* You assent, therefore, to their use, as books for the unlearned, as St. Gregory styles them: but you are scandalized at the reverence paid to them, by those who kiss them affectionately, bow their head to them, or prostrate themselves before them. All these usages, together with some others, more common among the Greeks, are to be judged of by the known intention and principles of those who practise them, and especially by the solemn declarations of the Church. The second Council of Nice,† whilst approving of them, expressly

* Vol. ii. p. 113. † Hard. Conc. Gen. t. iv. p. 455.

says that "supreme worship which is according to faith, and alone becomes the Divine Nature," must not be given to images. If you cannot understand, why an intellectual Christian may without sin kiss a crucifix, or prostrate himself before it, neither may you account for the fondness with which a son, in a foreign land, presses to his lips the miniature of a loved mother. St. Gregory, writing to Secundinus, who had asked for a picture of our Saviour, observes: "I know that you seek the image of our Saviour, not with a view of adoring it as God, but in order to have present to your mind the Son of God, and to excite His love in your heart, whilst you behold His image. We also prostrate ourselves before it, not as before the Deity, but we adore Him, whom by means of the image, we recall to mind in His birth, or passion, or seated on His throne."*

The fact of St. Epiphanius tearing down an image of some one, which he found hanging in a church, as if it were the image of Christ, or of a saint, tells rather in favor of the use of images, than against it, for he seems to have been indignant that the picture of some unknown person should occupy a place becoming only the image of our Lord, or some of His eminent servants. He accordingly promised to give one more suitable in its place.† This shows that his objection

* Ep. ad. Secundin. l. ix. p. 411. † Hopkins, vol. ii. p. 118.

regarded the particular picture in question, not the usage itself.

Dr. Milner justly availed himself of a fact recorded by Eusebius as an early instance of statuary being employed for religious purposes, namely, to commemorate a favor received from Christ. The historian testifies to the erection of two brazen statues at Edessa, in memory of the cure of the woman by the touch of the garment of our Saviour, and mentions without rejecting it, the prevalent persuasion, that persons were healed by the use of the plant which grew at the bottom, and rose to the fringe of the brazen cloak. He also states as notorious that paintings of Christ and of His Apostles Peter and Paul, were to be found. He accounts, indeed for this, from the usage existing among the heathen to raise statues to their benefactors. Nothing, however, is said by him condemnatory of the practice, as continued by them after their conversion, and applied to religious objects. His testimony is not brought forward to prove that pictures were then used in worship; but it shows conclusively that statues and paintings were already employed to represent sacred subjects.

Your mode of quoting testimonies is most unfair. You begin with Clement of Alexandria, who, you say, "thus speaks on the subject of images made for the purposes of religion, 'Those images which are made by vile and sordid men, are made of vain and useless materials; hence they are also vain, useless, material, and profane. Therefore, the works of art are by no means to be esteemed sacred and divine."* You conceal from your readers that the author is especially treating of heathen idolators, and you mutilate the text for this express purpose; it runs thus: "It is ridiculous, as the philosophers themselves say, for man, who is the sport of the gods, to make a god, and that God should be made after a ludicrous fashion; since the work is like its material, so that of ivory you have an ivory god; of gold, a golden one. Idols and temples which are made by vile men are formed of sluggish matter, so that they also are inert, material, and profane; and, however perfect the art, they partake of vileness. The works of art are not then sacred and divine."† The term ἀγάλματα *simulacra*, means idols, as the Lexicon explains it; it is generally used of statues of horses, oxen, or other animals, objects of idolatrous worship. You have left out altogether ἱερα *the temples.* I leave you to account for this dishonorable management.

St. Ambrose, whom you quote, moralizes on the fact related in Scripture, that Rachel hid the *Teraphim*, which she had taken from the house of her father. What these were it puzzles interpreters to divine, but the saint takes them for

* Vol. ii. p. 114.

† Stromat. l. vii. § v.

objects of idolatrous worship; and as he considers Rachel to be the type of the Church, he observes: "Holy Rachel, that is, the Church, or prudence, hid the idols (*simulacra*), because the Church knows not empty ideas and vain figures of idols; but she knows the true substance of the Trinity. Finally, she has abolished the shadow, and manifested the splendor of glory."* I am at a loss to know what force this passage can have against the use and veneration of Christian images. St. Ambrose spoke of the superstitious objects, or idols, which Rachel concealed, and he stated that the Church, having a knowledge by faith of the Divine Trinity, imparts it to her children, and leaves them not to seek God, as the heathens, in vain idols. Elsewhere he expresses the same sentiment: "Blessed Rachel, who, by her offspring took away our shame; blessed Rachel, who hid the worship and errors of the Gentiles, and declared that their idols are full of uncleanness."†

St. Augustin reproved most justly those who eat and drank to excess at the tombs of the dead, and practised certain superstitions, whom he calls worshippers of tombs, or of pictures; but he praised the picture of St. Stephen, which hung in the Church, where he pronounced the panegyric of the martyr: "This is a very sweet picture, where you see St. Stephen stoned, and

* De fuga saeculi, c. v. † De Jacob et beata vita, l. ii. c. v.

Saul in charge of the garments of those who stone him."*

Optatus relates that a report was spread by the Donatists, that on the arrival of Paul and Macarius, the imperial officers, who were expected to assist at the holy sacrifice, an image would be placed on the altar.† You infer that it was a sacred image; but from the official character which they bore, and the previous measures taken by them in the name of the Emperor, to repress the schism, there is great reason to believe that it was his portrait or arms. This rumor got coloring from the fact, that Macarius had condemned several Donatists for crimes against the public peace. However, it proved a false alarm, and all things proceeded as usual in the celebration of the sacrifice.

St. Gregory reproved Serenus, Bishop of Marseilles, for breaking a sacred image, on the pretext that it had become the occasion of superstitious worship, yet he commended his zeal, to prevent such abuse. You infer, thence, that he was averse to any of those marks of reverence which we now give to sacred pictures; but his words already cited prove the contrary. The contrast which you form between his teaching and that of the second Council of Nice, rests on an equivocal term, which by him is employed to

* Serm. cccxvi. alias xciv. de diversis.

† L. iii. de schismate Donat. sub finem.

denote supreme worship, whilst it is used by them of an inferior degree of worship, as they expressly state.

The very ancient custom which Tertullian attests, of representing Christ on the chalice under the image of the Good Shepherd,* is deemed unexceptionable by you; but you deny that it avails to establish the usage and veneration of images as now practised. It shows, however, that in the earliest times such representations were deemed suitable in connection with public worship, and in the immediate celebration of its highest mysteries. It is certain, also, from the examination of the catacombs, that they were made on the walls, on the sarcophagi, and in a great variety of ways; so that although they were chiefly designed for instruction as well as ornament, they prove that the usage of sacred pictures is most ancient. Every fact that establishes this usage serves to vindicate it in its present form, for the marks of respect shown to images are but a consequence of their being used in worship. If the Council of Elvire forbade "what is worshipped to be painted on the walls," it must have had local reasons to require this prohibition, which never was general, and can have no application to the circumstances of our times. Dr. Milner has clearly stated that the usage is purely disciplinary, and dependent on

* L. de pudicitia c. x.

the discretion of the Church, who, however, hurls her anathema against those who condemn it as implying idolatry or superstition.

The honor given to images is wholly referred to the objects represented by them, since in themselves they have no virtue or excellence. Hence the kissing of them, bowing to them, prostrating ourselves before them, or any like act of devotion, suggested by the piety of individuals, or prescribed in the solemn ritual of the Church, is to be regarded as directed to such object. Gardiner, Bishop of Winchester, under Henry VIII., in defending certain acts of respect then paid to sacred images, observed, that "if they had been used to be censed and to have candles offered unto them, none were so foolish to do it to stock or stone, or to the image itself, but it was done to God and His honor before the image."* The ritual of Good Friday directs that the Crucifix be uncovered, which during the preceding weeks had been veiled, and that as its arms are successively exposed, the faithful should be admonished by the celebrant, and invited to adore. "Behold the wood of the cross, on which the salvation of the world hung; come, let us adore." It is then laid on the steps of the altar, and the clergy, after three genuflexions, kiss the sacred image, which is subsequently honored in like manner by the

* Strype Eccl. Mem. p. 52.

people, or simply kissed by them at the communion railing, as is generally practised here. These are the most solemn acts which we perform, and the only acts which are specially prescribed, if we except the bowing to the cross by the priest, when he passes before it. The object of our adoration, as explained by St. Gregory, is the Saviour Himself. Dr. Milner pointed to the ceremony of bowing at the name of Jesus, which is practised by the members of the Church of England, as calculated to illustrate our usages in regard to the cross, and other sacred images. You reply that the name is no image. It is something less, it is a fleeting sound, directed nevertheless to represent the Saviour to our thoughts. You add that the worship is not given to the name, but to God, who alone can be the rightful object of worship. I trust you do not deny that our Redeemer, even as man, is rightfully worshipped, on account of the union of the human nature with the Divine in the second Divine Person. We then worship our Redeemer Himself, whom the image, like the sound, presents to our mind. "If the same argument could be pleaded for the images and relics of Rome, her advocates might claim a sure and easy victory."* These are your own words. The victory is ours.

The miraculous opening of the eyes of certain

* Vol. ii. p. 112.

images of the Virgin, which you ridicule, is to be judged of on principles of evidence. The Holy See is extremely cautious not to admit any miracle without satisfactory proof, so that if, as you assert, it allows even a local festival to be celebrated in commemoration of such a fact, there is the strongest presumption that the testimony has been found satisfactory. Nowhere in this age, are people so easily imposed on as not to be able to discover trickery and fraud, if it exist, in a matter which is public, and open to observation for a long period. Intelligent individuals and men hostile to religion are always found among the crowd of observers. When, then, thousands attest a fact such as that which you deride, I do not venture to reject it, lest I fall into scepticism with regard to facts of a still more extraordinary character recorded in the Divine writings. Yet, as the Church does not make such facts matters of necessary belief, I use no effort to bring my mind to positive assent, as long as the evidence is not brought under my view. Thus credulity and temerity are avoided. I am at no loss, however, to conceive why God may vouchsafe to give such extraordinary indications of His favor, at periods when impiety seems to triumph, to console and support His servants, by the reflection that their Mother and Advocate turns towards them eyes full of compassion, and pleads for them above, as also to manifest His approval of the devotion to her, which is assailed by the profane.

You do not, Right Reverend Sir, think it beneath you, to renew the charge of our omitting the second commandment, "while, in order to prevent the cheat from being discovered, they split," you say of us, "the Tenth Commandment into two."* All the words of the commandments, especially that appendage of the first, which you make a distinct commandment, are in our ordinary catechisms in use in this country, from the beginning, as well as in our larger catechisms, and the Bible. In the small catechisms of Europe, it was customary to give only the first words, that children might more easily commit them to memory. On this very reasonable custom that most unjust charge is based. You know that in the division of the commandments, we follow St. Augustin, and that the Lutherans agree with us. Even Cranmer, in the *catechismus* set forth under Edward, retained the same division.

You endeavor to fasten on Dr. Milner the charge, if not of forging a testimony, at least of producing it with full knowledge of its being a forgery. The passage was quoted more than a thousand years before his time, in the second General Council of Nice, as an extract from a letter of St. Basil to Julian the Apostate. To

* Vol. ii. p. 129.

prove that Dr. Milner knew it to be supposititious, as modern critics regard it, you state that in the Parisian edition which he used, "the heading of the very page on which it stands presents the title, 'Epistolæ Spuriæ.'" Give me leave to say, this is false. The extract begins, and the greater part of it is found on the preceding page. You express "renewed surprise that this Apostolic Vicar had descended to cite the false and pretended testimony of Basil, with the title Spurious Epistles, staring him in the face."* The title stared Dr. Milner in the face, only as a sign-board hanging on the opposite side of the way. The general heading under which this extract is given, includes some letters having no date, some of doubtful authenticity, and some certainly spurious. Various letters are then given without any particular brand. On the page following the one on which the extract commences, the title of 'Spurious Epistles' first appears. There is, then, no evidence to support your accusation. Yet you add: "Such is the Jesuitical morality, which deems it no sin to use a pious fraud for the sake of proselyting." What principle of morals can justify this wholesale calumny?

* Ib. p. 197.

LETTER XVI.

On the Primacy.

RIGHT REVEREND SIR:

AS you have not cared to substantiate your quotations, or sustain your reasonings on the Primacy, in detail, I must confine myself to those points on which you specially join issue. You maintain anew that πέτρος means a stone, whilst πέτρα means a rock, so that according to you, the text of St. Matthew, xvi. v. 18, runs thus: "Thou art a stone, and on this rock I will build my church." The utter want of connection in this mode of explaining the text, sufficiently shows its incongruity. You quote many passages of the Old Testament, to prove that God is called a rock, which you demonstrate by reference to the Hebrew term, literally rendered in the Protestant version. Your erudition, however, is thrown away in endeavoring to establish a distinction in the text of the promise, on account of the Greek terms, since it is certain that in the Syriac the same term is employed in both places. As this was the language which our Saviour used, there is no possibility of distinguishing what is so clearly identical. The most learned Protestant interpreters, English and German, as Bloomfield avows, have long since abandoned the distinction as untenable.

In the text of Luke xxi. 24, which you quote, our Lord checks the ambitious tendencies of His disciples, and inculcates humility as the necessary duty of the highest in authority: "He who is the greatest among you, let him be as the least." He also warns Simon to confirm his brethren, assuring him that He had prayed for him specially, that his faith might not fail. This you chose not to notice. Your other objections from Scripture, as well as that just solved, have been already met in my former work, so that I shall content myself with stating that Cave, the learned Anglican, acknowledges that Peter acted the chief part in the Council of Jerusalem. Grotius says that his epistles have an energy characteristic of the prince of the Apostles; and even Calvin admits that he appears as their leader.

You insist that Peter was not Bishop of Rome, because Irenæus says that "he delivered to Linus the episcopal right to govern it." Yet this may be understood of his directing him to take charge of it after his death, since the same writer says, that Clement, who succeeded Anaclitus, after Linus, was "third in succession from the Apostles;" which supposes that the chair was first filled by either of them. He ascribes the foundation of the Roman See to both Peter and Paul. No one imagines that St. Peter remained at Rome, or at Antioch, during the whole period assigned to his occupancy of either See. His special relation to the See did not abridge his apostolic authority, or prevent his attention to the Church at large.

Origen, when not indulging his usual fondness for mystical interpretation, as in the passages which you object, states distinctly that "supreme power to feed the sheep was given to Peter."*

Cyprian, in numberless passages, even in that which you quote, affirms that on "Peter the Church was built," and praises him for not having put forward his primacy to silence Paul, when reproved by him. You admit that "he appears to have adopted, to some extent, the notion which was now beginning to be maintained in favor of Roman supremacy."†

Eusebius testifies to the coming of Peter to Rome, and that Linus was the first to hold the episcopate after his martyrdom, which proves that during his lifetime, Rome had no bishop but himself.

St. Ambrose, in the passage which you object, speaks of Peter's faith as the foundation of the Church, referring especially to his belief in God Incarnate, as he is refuting the Arians. His privilege, he affirms, is communicated to each

* In Ep. ad Rom. lv. n. 10. † Vol. i. p. 450.

one who imitates his faith, since he also becomes as it were, a foundation of the Church, his example serving to support it, wherefore Ambrose adds: "If he cannot equal Peter, he can imitate him."* Such applications of the sacred text, which are common with the fathers, do not interfere with its literal meaning. Ambrose, in like manner, designates the faith of each one a rock, on which a spiritual edifice may be erected. When he teaches, that "what is said to Peter, is said to the Apostles,"† he means that the power to bind and loose is given to them likewise. He is there arguing against the Novatians, who denied to the Church the power of pardoning very heinous offences, which he justly insists was given to all the Apostles. He also says, that the operation of the Divine Trinity is not confined to Peter, since all the Apostles share in the great work of instructing and sanctifying mankind. He looked on the labors and virtues of Paul as equal to those of Peter, although he distinctly recognizes his special privilege as the foundation of the Church: "Paul was not inferior to Peter, although he is the foundation of the Church; the other is a skilful architect, who understands how to establish the steps of the nations who believe."‡ The other passage which you quote, as is your general practice, by re-

* L. vi. Luc. c. ix. † Enarr. in Ps. xxxviii.
‡ L. ii. de Sp. S.

ferring to the page and volume of a particular edition,* without specifying the work, is taken from a treatise on the Sacraments, which the learned critic Cellier denies to be the work of Ambrose. The sentiment it expresses is, however, a just one. The author, who is certainly very ancient and orthodox, declares his wishes to follow in all things the Roman Church; yet claims a right to adhere to a pious usage of the Church of Milan, although the same rite was not observed at Rome, namely the washing of the feet of the neophytes on their coming forth from the font: "We know well that the Roman Church, whose example and pattern we desire to follow in all things, has not this usage. I wish to follow the Roman Church in all things; yet we also as men have understanding, and therefore we are right in observing that which is elsewhere more properly practised. We follow the Apostle Peter himself; we imitate his devotion. What does the Roman Church reply to this? Peter, who was Bishop of the Roman Church, is our authority for this practice. Peter himself says: 'Lord, not my feet only, but my hands and head likewise.' "†

St. Jerom acknowledged Pope Damasus, the successor of St. Peter, to be the rock on which the Church was built, and implored his direction in regard to the terms to be used in speaking of

* Op. Ed. Bened. tom. 2, p. 664, § 158.
† L. iii de Sac. c. 1.

the mystery of the Trinity.* He recognized, indeed, each bishop, whether at Rome, or Eugubium, as having the same priesthood, but he did not ascribe to them the same governing authority, which would be manifestly in opposition to the testimony of all antiquity. He admits that the strength of the Church is consolidated upon all the Apostles; Peter, however, "being constituted head, that the occasion of schism may be taken away." Christ is called by him the foundation of the Church, laid by Paul the Apostle; but Peter also is the foundation, his name being derived from Him. The passage which you quote, to show that bishops and priests were originally the same, may please the Presbyterians; it does not help your cause as regards the Sovereign Pontiff. It may be plausibly employed to show that bishops are not of Divine institution, as perhaps you hold, since you regard them as not necessary for the being of the Church; but it does not interfere with the prerogative of the one great Apostle.

It may be sufficient to observe with St. Augustin, that "in the Roman Church the princedom of the Apostolic chair always flourished."† Instead of reciting anew passages from him and the other fathers, which you had already quoted in your former work, and I had explained in my reply, you should have shown that my explana-

* Ep. xv. Damaso. † Ad Glorium et Eleusium, Ep. xliii.

tions were not satisfactory, and you should have strengthened your former conclusions by new authorities or arguments. But as you are pleased to ignore what I so fully treated, I must beg again to refer to my larger work on the Primacy, where all is set forth in great detail.

Although you discover some commencement of Roman supremacy in the time of St. Cyprian, you date the origin of its appellate power from a decree of the Emperor Valentinian, A. D. 366. Yet the decree of the Council of Sardica, which recognized and regulated the proceedings in case of appeal, was prior to this date; and even before this council, appeals were made and received by Pope Julius and others. You observe, that if the right to receive them were divine, the imperial decree would have been unnecessary; you must, however, perceive that it served to enforce the action of the ecclesiastical tribunal, by giving it a civil sanction. The first Council of Constantinople, in regulating the relations of diocesan bishops, made no enactment regarding the Bishop of Rome; but undertook to invest the Bishop of Constantinople with privileges like those of the Roman Bishop, on account of the civil pre-eminence of the city. The words of the canon, as given by you, are: "The Bishop of Constantinople ought to have the primacy of honor with or after (Gr. μετα) the Bishop of Rome, because that is the New Rome." Notwithstanding that you are pained at small verbal criticisms, I must observe that the Greek preposition is determined to the latter signification, by the accusative case which follows it. The Council did not attempt to raise the Bishop of Constantinople to the rank of the Roman Bishop, but desired to give him the second place in the hierarchy, which seemed to them to be due to the imperial city. In stating that the fathers had given privileges to Rome as the seat of empire, the Council did not insinuate that such had been their chief motive; for they well knew that its power had been recognized under the Pagan emperors, and after it had ceased to be the capital. If it had originated from its civil greatness, it must have expired with the translation of the seat of empire. This council, in styling the See of Jerusalem the mother of all churches, had regard to its antiquity, not to its authority.

I am sorry to be obliged to charge you with a manifest misstatement of the proceedings at Chalcedon. You state truly, that the Papal Legates opposed the decree; and you represent Paschasius one of them as detected in the attempt to support it, by the fraudulent interpolation of the Nicene Canon, which he began in these words: "The Roman Church hath always had the Primacy." "The attempted fraud," you say, "was detected, and the true meaning given, which had no such words. The decree was accordingly confirmed in favor of the Church of

Constantinople; and we may readily imagine the expressions of indignation and contempt with which the impudent forgery was branded by the fathers."* This statement is altogether at variance with the facts. The privileges of the See of Rome were not at all called in question; but as the first Council of Constantinople, eighty years before, had framed a decree, giving to the bishop of that city the second place in the hierarchy, and the Oriental bishops at Chalcedon, in the preceding session, held in the absence of the legates, had confirmed it, omitting even some restrictions, which had been inserted by the fathers of Constantinople, to save, to some extent, the ancient prerogatives of Antioch and Alexandria, the legates complained of this proceeding, and desired that it should be reversed, as contrary to the Nicene Canon. The judges in the Council, who were civil officers charged with the maintenance of order, demanded that the legates and the friends of the See of Constantinople, should produce the canons; whereupon the Legate Paschasius read the sixth canon of Nice, beginning with the words above stated. A secretary of the Council was furnished with another copy by the archdeacon of the Church of Constantinople, which he accordingly read, without those prefatory words. No observation whatever was made as

* Vol. i. p. 464.

to the apparent discrepancy, because no question was raised as to the primacy of Rome. The only inquiry made by the judges was, whether the bishops had acted, in the preceding session, free from all restraint; which being affirmed by them, the judges pronounced sentence in these words: "From what has been done, and from the attestation given by each one, we consider, that before all, the primacy and eminent honor should be preserved, according to the canons, to the most beloved of God, archbishop of ancient Rome; but that it is proper that the most holy archbishop of the imperial city of Constantinople, the new Rome, should enjoy the same privileges of honor after him, and that he should have full power to ordain the metropolitans of Asia, Pontus, and Thrace."* From the very terms of this decree, it may be inferred that the reading of the canon by the Legate was approved of, since the very term τὰ πρώτεια is used in both places; and the latter is professedly grounded on previous canons. So far, then, from any charge of fraud being advanced, there is the strongest presumption that the reading was recognized as authentic. There is full evidence that no objection was raised, no question entertained as to the Roman primacy, which, on the contrary, was formally avowed. The great desire of the Eastern

* Conc. vol. ii. p. 642.

fathers was to give the imperial city like privileges, which they express by a different term: των ἀυτων πρέσβειων. These, although sometimes called equal ἴσων, were only such as were suitable to patriarchs, and were limited chiefly to three provinces. The opposition of the legates was owing to the instructions of the Pope, who was aware that an effort of the kind was likely to be made, which he ordered them to resist. The influence of the court was sufficient to induce the Oriental bishops to yield to the ambition of its favorite, the bishop of the capital; but nothing could move the Pontiff, who, deaf to the entreaties of the bishops, the emperor and the empress, by the authority of the Blessed Peter, annulled the canon, as an infraction of the order of the hierarchy, recognized by the first General Council. Your readers, Right Reverend Sir, may have been easily led by your insinuations, to imagine that expressions "of indignation and contempt" were uttered by the fathers; but there is no ground whatever for thinking so. They respectively sought to gain the assent of the legates to the measure, by showing that it was not wrung from the bishops, but willingly yielded for the honor of the Bishop of the imperial city. No forgery—no interpolation whatever, was alleged. The Roman primacy was distinctly acknowledged, not merely on the ground of the civil pre-eminence which Rome had once enjoyed, as insinuated in the decree, but because "the care of the vineyard was intrusted by our Lord to Leo in the person of Peter," as the fathers distinctly state in their letter to the Pontiff. Could you discover in Dr. Milner any similar misstatement, you would have reason to reproach him, as you most unwarrantably do elsewhere, with "dishonest insinuation, gross deception, and unmeasured reliance on the prejudices of his hearers."

The effort which you have made to revive the exploded tale of the Popess Joan, deserves the praise of ingenuity, though not of good judgment or candor. The disgusting details into which you enter so minutely, shall not be handled by me, for I have no fears that the succession will, on this account, be called in question, whilst Bayle, Gibbon, and Blondell, with the host of writers of the present day, reject the absurd story, which is disproved by known facts and dates. Besides, as the English bishops, at the time of the alleged intrusion of a Popess, about the middle of the ninth century, and for nearly seven hundred years afterwards, were in communion with Rome, and derived their jurisdiction from it, nothing can weaken the succession without involving your claims in still greater uncertainty. The learned Bishop Beveridge felt this, when he observed: "We do not deny that the apostolical succession hath been continued in the Church of Rome."* This re-

* Serm. 1, Christ's presence with His ministers, p. 24, vol. i.

flection should have made you pause, before asserting that the Pope is Antichrist, since you necessarily derive under him, if at all. Grotius lamented that any Protestants should have broached this impiety. That you should adopt it, betrays a desperate resolution to overturn the Papal chair at any hazard; but there it stands in its lofty position. Whilst men, frenzied by passion, gnash their teeth and blaspheme, the alleged Antichrist repeats forever the divinely inspired profession of Peter: "Thou art Christ, the Son of the living God." He proclaims at all times the mandate of the Father, that at the name of Jesus all should bow in homage—those who are in heaven, on earth, or in the lowest depths of hell.

Your ingenuity discovers "a trick" and "a bold scheme of pious fraud attempted in the service of Papal ambition," in the proceedings in regard to appeals to the Holy See from the African clergy, in the early part of the fifth century. Apiarius, a priest, excommunicated by Urban, Bishop of Sicca, appealed to Pope Zosimus, who soon despatched two priests, as his legates, with powers to restore the appellant, excommunicate the Bishop if he refused to submit to their decision, and regulate all appeals for the future in accordance with the Nicene Canons. It is now certain that the canons thus referred to were not enacted at Nice, but in a council held at Sardica, some twenty years after that of Nice; yet at

Rome they were called Nicene, and were contained in the same volume with those of Nice, as even the Jansenist Quesnel confessed on inspection of a very ancient Vatican manuscript. As the interval between the two councils was so small, and many of the same prelates were present at both, it easily happened that the canons of Sardica were regarded as a sequel and supplement to those of Nice. Innocent I., the predecessor of Zosimus, often refers to them under this appellation. In Africa, however, they were wholly unknown, and the fathers therefore hesitated to adopt them as a permanent basis of action until their authenticity should be ascertained by special messengers sent to examine the archives of the great churches of Alexandria, Antioch, and Constantinople. Their report was unfavorable, inasmuch as the canons were not found in those churches, so that the Council expostulated respectfully with the Pontiff, and prayed him not to lend a ready ear to the complaints of clergymen refractory to the authority of their immediate superiors. On these facts you build your charges of trickery and fraud, although the canons are now universally acknowledged to have been enacted at Sardica, and consequently to have the same weight and authority as if they had proceeded from the Nicene fathers. A mere misnomer is the only pretext for so grave an accusation. The African fathers showed the most marked deference for the Papal authority, since they submitted to it at once in the case in question; and on the report apparently adverse to their authenticity, they limited themselves to respectful remonstrance and entreaty.

What you regard as an impious fraud of Pope Stephen, was certainly no more than a rhetorical fiction, which Pepin must have perfectly understood, when the letter in the name of St. Peter the Apostle, urging him to come to the relief of Rome, his favored city, was sent to him by the Pontiff. It is incredible that even in the eighth century, or in any other age, however credulous, a prince so distinguished could have been imposed on by a fraud so destitute of probability.

The scandals given by certain occupants of the Papal chair, are a fruitful theme of reproach, on which you delight to expatiate; yet if we consider the turbulence of the times, the total disorganization of society, the temporary ascendency obtained at Rome by some petty potentates, the national partialities which favored some intruders, through jealousy of German influence, we shall not be astonished that in the tenth and eleventh centuries some instances occurred of wicked and ambitious men, who seized on the reins of government. Few, very few, were those who deserved to be marked with the brand of infamy. Towards the close of the fifteenth century, and in the early part of the sixteenth, two or three Pontiffs appeared with the evidences of early frailty near their persons; and it must be avowed that they scarcely atoned for it by fervor and devotedness, one perhaps excepted. Of Alexander VI. few have ventured to speak, even in extenuation of censure; but, although I feel convinced that his vices have been exaggerated, and that crimes have been laid to his charge without any just grounds, still I have no plea to offer for his licentiousness, first indulged, it is said, when a young officer of the army, but continued, I doubt not, under the mantle of the Roman purple, and shamelessly avowed, when he sat on high, in that chair, whose occupant is styled "Holiness," to remind him of the sanctity which becomes his station.

The character of several Popes has suffered unjustly from the interested misrepresentations of rivals, or their partisans, as also of the adherents of schismatical emperors and kings. National jealousies led the Italians to satirize the French popes who sat at Avignon, while the French viewed with no partiality several who sat at Rome. The civil relations of the Pontiff to his subjects have often cast odium on the exercise of his ecclesiastical authority, and his political associations with various princes have contributed in no slight degree to excite the rancor, and provoke the animadversions of writers of other nations. Certain historians assume the air of candor, by reciting the very words of some contemporary, who has recorded his view of the personal character, or public acts of an individual Pope, without reflecting that he may have mistaken rumors for facts, and followed the bias of partisanship to the prejudice of truth and justice. I feel it unnecessary to enter into a detailed vindication of the various pontiffs, whose character is more generally the object of attack; but I fearlessly say, that considering the long succession of Popes, the convulsions of society, the vicissitudes of Rome, and the endless variety of circumstances in which the Popes have been placed, it is nothing short of a miracle that, in general, their character has been pure and exalted, whilst their succession has been inviolably maintained. I take leave, then, Right Reverend Sir, to remind you of the course of argument pursued by St. Augustin, when Petilian, the Donatist, made light of the boast of Catholics, that they enjoyed the communion of the See of Peter, which he impiously called the chair of pestilence, unfit for saints to occupy. St. Augustin replied to the insult: "Do you not feel that this is not argument, but wanton contumely? You make this allegation without proving it; and if even you proved it as to some individuals, you could not, on their account, prejudice the claims of others. Nevertheless, if all throughout the world were such as you most wantonly charge, what has the chair of the Roman Church done to you—in which Peter sat, and Anastasius sits at present? or the chair of the Church of Jerusalem, in which James sat, and in which at this day John is sitting, with which we are connected in Catholic unity, and from which you are separated in wicked frenzy? Why do you call the apostolic chair a chair of pestilence? If it be on account of the men who you suppose propound the law without fulfilling it, did the Lord Jesus Christ, on account of the Pharisees, of whom He said, 'They say, and do not,' dishonor, in any way, the chair on which they sat? Did he not commend that chair of Moses, and rebuke them without prejudice to the chair? For He says, 'They sit on the chair of Moses; the things which they say, do ye; but do not the things which they do; for they say and do not.' If you would reflect on these things, you would not dishonor the apostolic chair, whose communion you have not, on account of the men whom you slander. But what else is this, unless to show oneself at a loss for something to say, and yet to be able to utter nothing but contumely?"*

Boniface VIII. may fairly be given as an instance of the injustice which some Popes have suffered from the partisans of crowned heads. His learning and talent are unquestionable; but his bold resistance to Philip the Fair, in his aggression on the rights of the clergy, and in the oppression of his subjects, exposed him to the royal resentment. To re-

* Contra lit. Petilian. l. ii. n. 118.

lieve the king from the shame and odium of his maltreatment of the Pontiff, who died in consequence of it, it was reported by the king's adherents, that Boniface was an atheist, and that after his humiliation, he had yielded to despair. Happily for the cause of truth, his body, after three hundred years' repose, being identified, was found in an admirable state of preservation, as if Heaven would signify its approval of a faithful and virtuous prelate. The process against his memory proved a failure, and the General Council of Vienne, not long after his death, pronounced him orthodox. You, nevertheless, reopen the cause, produce anew the witnesses, whose testimony was rejected as perjured, or irrelevant, and after a mock tria' find him guilty of atheism and infidelity. This is more ridiculous than painful, especially since you pathetically expatiate on the awful condition of the Roman Church at that period, inasmuch as a Cardinal and a Pope "both were downright atheists."* The name of the Cardinal which you give, is Cajetan; the Pope, Boniface—who were one and the same person. This curious blunder is repeated several times with the like expressions of horror and commiseration!

* Vol. i. p. 142, 144, 339.

LETTER XVII.

On Temporal Power.

Right Reverend Sir:

YOU count for nothing Dr. Milner's disclaimer of any civil or temporal supremacy in the Pope, by which he can depose princes; and you make light of the oath of the English and Irish Catholics, both prelates and people, who deny that "he hath, or ought to have any temporal or civil jurisdiction, power, superiority, or pre-eminence, directly, or indirectly, within the realm." This you consider to be "ingeniously worded to gull the British Parliament," and you avow that "this is a kind of jurisdiction which was never demanded by the highest advocate of Ultramontanism." I thank you for this avowal, which is calculated to remove some of the odium which has been cast on the views of certain divines, who favored the opinion, which has long ceased to be advocated even in Rome itself. I never before suspected that the British Parliament, with Pitt at its head, was altogether gullible. It is clear that if you had been there to enlighten them, the Catholics would still remain unemancipated.

You will scarcely venture to deny, that there are circumstances in which the rights of sovereigns over their subjects cease, in consequence of the enormous abuse of power. In such cases, when the European nations were generally Catholic, the Pope was looked up to, as the proper authority to declare this forfeiture. By the force of circumstances these nations coalesced into a federal alliance, or republic, of which he was the acknowledged head. You deny this, which, however, is affirmed not only by Voltaire, but by our own jurists, Kent, Wheaton, and other respectable authorities. Voltaire expressly says: "The nations belonging to the Roman communion appeared to be one great republic."* Chancellor Kent, speaking of the middle ages, observes: "The Church had its councils or convocations of the clergy, which formed the nations professing Christianity into a connection resembling a federal alliance, and those councils sometimes settled the titles and claims of princes, and regulated the temporal affairs of the Christian powers. The confederacy of the Christian nations was bound together by a sense of common duty and interest in respect to the rest of mankind."† Wheaton says, that "during the middle ages, the Christian States of Europe began to unite and to acknowledge the obligation of an international law common to all those

* Essai sur l'Histoire Générale, t. ii. ch. xlviii.

† Commentaries on American Law, by James Kent, New York, 1836, part i. lect. i. p. 9, 10.

who professed the same religious faith."* This sufficiently accounts for the interposition of the Pope in regard to Sovereigns, apart from positive and formal concessions. The recognition of the Christian religion as the supreme rule of all the members of this confederacy, naturally led to appeal to the judgment of the Pontiff, in cases where the relative rights of princes in regard to one another, or their rights over their subjects, were in question. When the obligation of an oath was to be defined, he was considered most competent to declare how far it extended, and his declaration was accepted as a safe guide to delicate consciences. You deny that he only interfered upon the application of the people; yet it is certain that in the very first instance on record, the Saxons had appealed to Alexander II., the predecessor of Gregory VII., and to this Pontiff himself against the tyranny of Henry, long before the sentence of deposition was pronounced. "The Pope," you say, "claimed that his office invested him with the sovereignty of the world, as the Vicar of Christ, by the divine decree, and not by the will of princes or people." I have never met with any proof of such pretensions. Gregory repeatedly acknowledged that Henry was placed by Divine Providence in the pinnacle of power.†

* Elements of International Law, Pref. to third edition.

† "Tibi, quem Deus in summo culmine rerum posuit." Apud Voigt, vol. i. p. 410; vol. ii. p. 57.

He, indeed, claimed and exercised the power of deposing the prince, who, he alleged, "was guilty of crimes so enormous as to deserve not only to be excommunicated, but according to all divine and human laws, to be deprived of the royal dignity." The Saxons had, in fact, already unanimously declared him dethroned for his crimes, and chosen Rudolph of Suabia to reign in his stead, in a meeting held 1073, at Gerstungen, after three days' deliberation; and although this measure did not take effect, and they were forced by the fortune of war to submit to his domination, they appealed anew in 1076 to Gregory, as the only one who could check his tyranny and cruelty. As he had not been crowned Emperor, they besought the Pope to exercise his power by setting aside the claims of Henry. In passing the sentence, Gregory appealed to the words of Christ, empowering Peter to loose and to bind, because his act was specially directed to the releasing of the people from the oath of allegiance; but from the previous allegations of crime and unworthiness, it is manifest that he relied on these for his justification. His authority had been invoked by both parties, and he exercised it, determining by his judgment the extent of the obligations of conscience in their mutual relations sanctioned by oath. The fathers of American Independence declared the oath of allegiance taken to the

British King, to be no longer binding, and without any pretensions to authority, they declared the people absolved from it, relying solely on the fact, that the correlative duty of protection and just government had been manifestly violated. The Pope grounded his sentence on far more flagrant abuses of power than are alleged in the Declaration of Independence. The difference between the middle ages and the present age is not in the principle, that the abuse of power causes its forfeiture, which is still maintained; or in the idea that the Church can interfere with the just exercise of civil authority, which was never asserted. Gregory himself says: "What regards the service and allegiance due to the king, we by no means wish to oppose or impede."* It lies in this, that a religious sanction was then given to the natural duty of allegiance, and was sought for the exercise of natural right in resisting oppression; whilst now men act on their own sense of right. The fact that the nations owed their civilization to the influence of religion, accounts for the difference.

You are mistaken in asserting that "it was simply a struggle between the Pope and the Emperor for the right of investiture." This was doubtless a highly important matter, intimately connected with the purity of the prelacy, and involving great civil consequences, but the docu-

* Ep. v. 5, quoted in Vie de Gregoire VII. vol. ii. p. 253, note du traducteur.

ments prove that unbridled licentiousness and wanton tyranny concurred to call forth the censures of the Pontiff.

The Bull of St. Pius V. deposing Elizabeth, shows that he shared the views of former Pontiffs in regard to his power. The old principle of English law, which made the maintenance of the Catholic faith a condition for holding the crown, as the profession of Protestantism is at present, was considered to be still in force, since her immediate predecessor had restored England to the communion of the Holy See. She is throughout styled "the pretended queen of England," because her right to the throne was regarded as null, on account of her illegitimacy, which stood declared on the statute book. Yet the plenary authority which the Pontiff claimed, regarded the government of the Church; and in this sense only does he allege that Christ made Peter prince over all people and kingdoms, "that he may preserve his faithful people in the unity of the spirit." The terms "to pluck up, to destroy, to scatter, to consume," which are borrowed from the Prophet Jeremiah, regard all acts of spiritual authority directed to extirpate error and vice. Doubtless Pius believed that in declaring Elizabeth a pretendant, and directing her pretensions to be disregarded, he was but stating authoritatively what the facts of the case warranted; for even he did not claim an absolute and arbitrary right to interfere in matters of this nature. Elizabeth, however, had possession of the throne, and succeeded in retaining it during a long reign, despite of his sentence. His act or views cannot prove what are the sentiments now generally entertained by Catholics; for if, as you acknowledge, the English Catholics continued to obey Elizabeth notwithstanding her deposition, and the martyred Campion on the scaffold proclaimed her queen, it may well be presumed that Catholics, at this day, are equally disposed to practise allegiance to their rulers. Sixtus V. was the last Pope who attempted to exercise this power, by renewing the sentence against Elizabeth, and issuing a similar one against the King of Navarre. More than two centuries have passed away, without any similar effort; for Pius VII., to whom you refer, only deprived Napoleon of the communion of the Church; which was certainly an exercise of spiritual authority. What you allege of his having absolved all Frenchmen from their obedience to Louis XVIII., was a simple recognition of the existing government of Napoleon, in which the nation had already acquiesced. When, in his Bull excommunicating the Emperor, he speaks of his own sceptre, he means his spiritual authority, which in its nature is far superior to that which is temporal, as Divine things are to human. In negotiations with the Emperor, he made no difficulty, in regard to that article of the Declaration, which affirms the independence of the civil power, although he was inflexibly opposed to the four Articles collectively, as his predecessors had been, as emanating from an assembly under the royal influence, and as a premature attempt to determine points, not yet decided by the supreme authority of the Church. You assert that the Pope, "as the *sole* vicar of Christ, that paramount master of the world, claims, in his own person, the authority of God, and saith, '*By me* kings reign, and princes execute judgment.' "* The manner of introducing this text,† and the use of italics, naturally convey the idea that the Pope applies these words to himself, in order to express his supreme power over princes; yet I have never met with any such application of it, and until you produce or refer to the document, I must regard it as your ingenious device. I find that St. Gregory VII., writing to Harold, King of Denmark, exhorts him to govern with justice and wisdom, adding "that of thee, the true Wisdom, which is God, may say: 'By me doth this king reign.'" You blame Dr. Milner for not giving the various views of divines on this subject. I believe there is no real difference at this day, for I do not know that the most devoted to the Holy See, claim for it any right of interference in secular concerns in the actual state of society; whilst I

* Vol. ii. p. 389. † Prov. viii. 15.

am persuaded that there is a very general disposition to regard the acts of former Popes, during the middle ages, as fully justified by the principles of jurisprudence then prevailing, and by the general consent of princes and nations, and as fraught with great benefits to society.

Mr. Brownson, with his usual independence, has ventured to seek the solution of the problems presented by the history of the middle ages, in a principle which was put forward by St. Gregory VII., and by the great defender of the indirect power, Bellarmin. He relies on the natural subordination of the temporal to the spiritual. As far as the middle ages are concerned, I conceive that this is satisfactory, because, in fact, that principle was then admitted and applied, and thus it necessarily entered into the compact between sovereigns and their subjects. The prince, at his coronation, swore to maintain the rights and privileges of the Church, of which he was the acknowledged protector, and the people regarded his fidelity to this trust as his most solemn duty. When he became a persecutor of religion, he violated the first condition on which he reigned, and exposed himself to ecclesiastical censures, which, by general law, were followed by the forfeiture of civil rights, if not removed within a year. If Queen Victoria were to profess the Catholic faith, you know, Right Reverend Sir, that she would forfeit her throne, because she is sworn to support the

Church as by law established. Her Protestant subjects would at once feel themselves released from their allegiance, as soon as her profession of Catholicity was placed beyond doubt. Can it be a matter of surprise, that Catholic nations exacted from their rulers a pledge to maintain their religion, and the rights of the Church, and made it a prominent article in the Great Charter of their rights and liberties? Those who approve of the English Bill of Rights, and Act of Settlement, cannot consistently condemn the policy of the nations generally in the middle ages, or wonder that when the coronation-oath was flagrantly violated, the oath of allegiance was declared no longer obligatory. The declaration of the Pope served rather to prevent the breach of allegiance, on grounds not sufficiently weighty to dissolve the obligation. This, however, does not concern us in the United States, since by the General Constitution there is no state-religion, and the Constitutions of the respective States guarantee liberty of conscience. The effort which is now made by a formidable party, to disturb these amicable relations, can derive no coloring or pretext from a theory, applicable only to the confederacy of Catholic nations as it subsisted in former ages, and which, after all, is only the speculation of an individual as to the causes of these historical phenomena. Although I addressed this distinguished publicist, in 1846, in terms of high commendation of his zeal and ability in defence of the Catholic faith, which he had embraced but two years before, and the other bishops concurred with me, none of us thought of rendering ourselves responsible for whatever views he might afterwards entertain, as he himself has recently avowed most distinctly, to correct the abuse made of our signatures, which are represented as implying an unqualified endorsement of all his sentiments.* Most assuredly I dissent from him, if he claim for the Pope any right to interfere with our civil allegiance. With his full knowledge and entire approval, Catholics everywhere pledge and render it to the Government under which they live; knowing that it is a duty independent of all ecclesiastical sanction. However strong may be the language sometimes employed by Mr. Brownson, I am convinced that he does not mean any such thing, and that he, as well as every other Catholic in the States, in the hour of trial will be found the devoted supporter of our National and State institutions.

Dr. Nevin acknowledges the advantages of the power exercised by the Popes in the middle ages: "The barbarians bowed to the authority of this power, as the only one that carried in it any principle of order, or that offered any promise of stability. Where all was chaos, there could be properly no usurpation. The right to

* Church Review, April, 1855.

rule fell where there was ability to rule. It is dishonest to try such times by the standard of a settled and well-ordered social state. The power to regenerate society, in the middle ages, lay wholly in the Church. On her devolved accordingly, as by Divine commission, the sovereign care of society and the duty of training it for its proper destiny."*

* Mercersburg Review, March, 1851, art. Modern Civilization.

LETTER XVIII.

On Abuses.

RIGHT REVEREND SIR:

TEN letters of your first volume, filling above two hundred pages, contain a summary of events which occurred from the commencement of the Church down to the time of the so-called Reformation. With the view of justifying this revolt on the plea of enormous corruption among the rulers of the Church and her clergy generally, you have gathered together all the scandals and disorders of which you could find traces in history. Fleury has given you the chief materials. His testimony you hold to be conclusive against Catholics, as he himself was a Catholic; but this circumstance does not give weight to his statements beyond what the documents, on which he relies, demand. It is, however, unnecessary to examine the facts in detail, since, even allowing disorders to have been as general and as enormous as he has painted them, they can furnish no argument against a Divine institution, whose Founder warned His followers that scandals must come, and pronounced woe to the world because of scandals. These cannot justify revolt against authority, which is necessarily grounded not on the personal merits of those who exercise it, but on the will of Christ, who imparted it. St. Augustin admonishes us: "When, either through the neglect of prelates, or by some necessity, or through unknown causes, we find that wicked persons are in the Church, whom we cannot correct or restrain by ecclesiastical discipline, let not the impious and destructive presumption enter our heart that we should imagine ourselves obliged to separate from them."*

All scandals and excesses should be put to the charge of human frailty and perversity. The authority of the Church rests on the commission given by Christ, which is unqualified and perpetual. I must claim the right to apply here a reflection suggested by Butler, the learned author of the Analogy, as an answer to the same objection urged by unbelievers against the Christian religion: "It may, indeed, I think truly be said, that the good effects of Christianity have not been small, nor its supposed ill effects, any effects at all of it, properly speaking. Perhaps, too, the things themselves done have been aggravated; and if not, Christianity hath been often only a pretence, and the same evils, in the main, would have been done, upon some other pretence. However great and shocking as the corruptions and

* S. Aug. l. de fide et operibus, c. v.

abuses of it have really been, they cannot be insisted upon as arguments against it, upon principles of theism. For one cannot proceed one step in reasoning upon natural religion any more than upon Christianity, without laying it down as a first principle, that the dispensations of Providence are not to be judged of by their perversions, but by their genuine tendencies; not by what they do actually seem to effect, but what they would effect, if mankind did their part—that part which is justly put and left upon them."*

The prevalence of concubinage among the clergy in some countries and some ages is a melancholy evidence of human weakness, and of the want of vigilance and zeal on the part of the prelates of the Church, some of whom gave the most scandalous examples. Yet we must take into consideration that what is branded as concubinage by St. Peter Damiani, and other strenuous advocates of Church discipline, was regarded by many as a state of wedlock;† the marriage, although originally unlawful, being regarded by many as valid. Cranmer is, therefore, said to have been twice *married*, in violation of his collegiate and priestly obligations. You can scarcely reject this plea, which at the time was put forward by the priests, and supported by

* The Analogy of Religion, by Joseph Butler, Bishop of Durham; part ii. ch. i.

† See Vie et Pontificat du Pape Gregoire VII. par J. Voight, traduite par l'Abbe Jager, vol. i p. 143.

jurists, on which account the efforts of various Popes to re-establish the ancient discipline, met with strong opposition. Viewed in this light, the relaxed state of clerical morals loses much of its revolting character, since it implies no more than the freedom of marriage, which ministers of every sect now enjoy. The Popes, however, especially Gregory, resisted the attempt to legalize the union, employed the censures of the Church, invoked the aid of the civil authorities, and even enlisted the zeal of the laity, generally, to break up the usage, destroy all appearance of prescription against the law of celibacy, and enforce the canonical observance. It would be a great mistake to suppose that at any time, or in any country, vice was so far dominant, as to leave the Church without worthy priests to minister at her altars. In the worst of times there were illustrious examples of purity and perfection in the sanctuary and in the cloister; and often when discipline became relaxed in a particular country, it was in a flourishing condition in other portions of the Church. Wars, civil dissensions, the intrusion, by emperors and kings, of their courtiers and dependents, into seats of authority, and the general degradation and partial barbarism which prevailed from various causes, concurred to produce relaxation; but there was still remaining a deep sense of the holiness that became the priesthood, and a reforming power, which finally raised them from the depth into which they had sunk. Had the Popes yielded in despair to the overwhelming torrent, and legalized these disorders by their positive sanction, History would not have had to record crimes so revolting; but neither would she have inscribed on her pages the brilliant virtues and glorious achievements of the apostolic men, who at all times shed lustre on the Church. The English schism was not, in the first instance, directed against clerical celibacy, on the contrary, Henry VIII. was entirely opposed to the marriage of the clergy, which was expressly proscribed in one of his six articles; and Elizabeth viewed it with no favor. In her reign it was regarded as illegal, so that Parker and others sought letters of legitimation for their children. In the diocess of Bangor, for some years after her accession, it was usual for the clergy to pay the bishop for a license to keep a concubine!* Elizabeth, of her own authority, suspended Fletcher, Bishop of London, only for marrying "a fine lady, and a widow."†

Married clergymen are less exposed to suspicion and censure than the professors of celibacy, but not less liable to temptation, whilst they are scarcely qualified to perform the high duties of the Christian priesthood. Due regard to the temporal interests and safety of their families, prevents them from making the heroic sacrifices, which at all times, but especially in seasons of

* Strype's Whitgift, p. 458. † Strype's Parker, p. 203.

danger and distress, are expected from the ministers of Christ. It is not wonderful that they abandon the confessional, and deny the daily sacrifice, for they cannot hope to possess the confidence of the bruised heart, and they dare not consecrate the Body which is from the Virgin. Pestilence scares them from the couch of the dying, to whom they have no mystic unction to afford. In their habits, views, and pursuits, they are like other men, only careful to observe certain rules of decorum suitable to their peculiar station. When will they produce an Apostle like Xavier, a benefactor of humanity such as Vincent of Paul, a martyr of zeal like Borromeo?

In regard to all the disorders and crimes which history attests, I have only to say with St. Augustin: "The Church is not defiled by the sins of men, since being spread throughout the whole world, according to the most faithful prophecies, she awaits the end of the world, as the shore, on reaching which she is at length rid of the bad fish, which being contained within the nets of the Lord, she bore their annoyance without fault, as long as she could not rid herself of them without impatience."*

Simony is one of those vices against which St. Gregory VII., St. Peter Damiani, and other holy prelates, inveighed with great earnestness, employing all their power and influence for its

* Contra Petil. l. iii. n. 43.

extirpation. It chiefly regarded bishoprics, abbeys, and benefices in general, which, as they had revenues attached to them, the Emperor granted to his favorites on the payment of a large sum to the royal treasury. By this means the wealthy and the ambitious occupied seats of honor in the Church, without possessing the virtues which should adorn her ministers. It was, indeed, a great source of scandal and disorder. Yet the Church of England does not view with such horror, certain practices which bear a close resemblance to it, such as the purchase of livings; advertisements for their sale, setting forth the revenue and other advantages, being frequent in the public papers. The opposition of the Popes to the practice of investiture, by the delivery of ring and crozier, arose partly from its connection with simoniacal traffic of this kind, and partly from the apparent communication of spiritual power by these symbols. There would have been little occasion for the inflamed invectives of holy men, if the standard of clerical morals had been reduced to the present level of the Church of England. Livings might have been sold, without a suspicion of simony; marriage might have thrown its mantle over human frailty; and kings or their ministers might have bestowed sacred offices, without appearing to trespass on hallowed ground.

The military character which attached to some bishops of the middle ages, cannot fairly be judged of, without taking into consideration their social position, and the general spirit of the age. Under the feudal system many of them had secular attributions, having vassals dependent on them. The warlike spirit of the Northmen, who had overspread the southern portions of Europe, had descended to their children, not wholly divested of its ferocity, and as society was split up into numberless sections, each baron being the head of his vassals, dissensions easily arose, and in the absence of legal tribunals, the appeal to the sword was frequent. The want of regular civil process led to the enforcement of right by military display, and as the jarring claims of certain bishops and abbots to jurisdiction, or to precedence, involved civil rights and privileges, they were sometimes supported and enforced by their respective vassals, in sanguinary contests. Elections to the vacant chair of Peter, were often attended or followed by bloody strife, the partisans of some ambitious aspirant using force, which the friends of the lawful claimant were under the necessity of repelling. Church prelates, like other feudal lords, were obliged to send their vassals to the support of the lord paramount, and were often required to appear in person on the battle-field, although they were not obliged themselves to take part in the contest. I am not disposed to deny that those ages were marked by many acts of cruelty and barbarity, which at this day must excite amazement—such as the frequent scooping out of the eyes—the cutting out of the tongue—the mutilation of ears and nose—and various other punishments of a revolting character. I admit that some bishops displayed rather the bravery of the soldier, than the mild virtues of their office, which, considering the general temper of the times, is scarcely a matter of wonder. The civilization of those nations could not be perfected in a moment; it was progressing gradually, and almost imperceptibly by the application of the Christian maxims to daily life. Their influence, even on the clergy, was not instantaneous and absolute. These were taken from the midst of their countrymen, whose sentiments and dispositions they shared. It was much to restrain them within certain limits. By degrees they became imbued with the meek spirit of their Divine Model, and successfully exerted their influence to promote peace and order. Dr. Nevin, the learned President of Marshall College, having stated that the Church was intrusted by Providence, with the task of reforming and training the nations, asks: "Was this providential trust, then, abused in its actual administration? Did the Church exercise her guardianship over the infant nations of Europe, in such a way as, instead of assisting, to repress their upward tendencies—in such a way as to retard rather than to advance their progress in true civilization? We have seen already that she was a fountain of order and law; that she brought society into regular and settled form; that she caused the wilderness to become a fruitful field; that she curbed the passions of men, and set bounds to their violence; that she led them to dwell in families, and to cultivate the domestic virtues; that she inoculated manners with a new spirit of gentleness and peace; that she raised the standard of morality, and purified the public conscience far beyond all that was known in the ancient world; that she established a reign and fashion of benevolence, such as had not previously entered the wildest dreams of philanthropy. We have seen all this, and have felt that a power so employed could not well be at war with the best interests of humanity.*"

Among the exaggerations of the evils of those times I must point to your account of the disorders of the University of Paris, in the thirteenth century. It is taken professedly from Fleury, who recites the words of a cotemporary author, and gives the enactments made to remedy them. So far you are sustained by evidence; yet you make a strange mistake in translating the historian, which gives a false coloring to the whole statement, and affords you matter for much comment. The Papal Legate who visited the University, complained that the students on

* Mercersburg Review, March, 1851, art. Modern Civilization.

certain festivals broke through all restraint, and among other things in the very churches, in which they should assemble to celebrate the divine office, played at dice on the altars, *on which the Body and Blood of Christ are consecrated.* You translate it: "on which they consecrate;" mistaking altogether the force of the French phrase, "*on consacre.*" Excuse this small verbal criticism. Thus you make them all priests, and instead of a college outbreak on a festival in which the vigilance of Superiors was relaxed, you actually charge the professors and priests as guilty of habitual profanation of the altars on which they offered up the Victim of our ransom. The fact in question is difficult to conceive, but it possibly may have been connected with some of those strange plays which were in vogue in the middle ages. You give a frightful picture of the morals of the students; but you might have somewhat relieved its shades, by some contrary examples of virtue. You might also have reflected, that where thousands of youth from all nations were gathered together, great disorders might be naturally expected. Most probably they had not College Proctors traversing the streets of Paris, as now at Oxford, even in open day, to watch the behavior of the students. It was the glory of the Popes to foster education everywhere, by great privileges bestowed on those who frequented the schools of the University, as it was their care to interpose their authority to repress disorders. That of Paris had many holy youths within its walls, some of whom like Innocent III. rose to the highest dignity; others are now on the calendar of saints. When occasionally disorder manifested itself, it was punished and corrected. Under Innocent, four of the professors, distinguished for learning and piety, with a number of the students, retired to a valley in the diocese of Langres, and there devoted themselves to contemplation and other exercises of piety. It is fair to counterbalance evil with good in estimating the moral influence of an institution.

You have studiously kept out of view the brilliant examples of virtue with which the history of the Church abounds, and seldom referred to them unless to caricature and mock them. Yet even they give but a faint idea of the amount of good which at all times was practised, since vice is of itself more forward and remarkable, whilst virtue courts secresy, and desires no witness or approver but God. St. Augustin, when reproached by the Donatists with the scandals of Catholics, observed that the wicked are like chaff raised on high and driven about by the wind, whilst the good are as wheat, lying concealed on the threshing-floor. "Let us not imagine that the good are few in number; they are many, but they lie concealed amidst a great multitude; for we cannot deny that the wicked are in greater number, so that the good are scarcely discernible among them, as the grains of wheat are not perceptible on the threshing-floor. A man who looks on the threshing-floor, may imagine that all is mere chaff; yet there is a quantity of grain there to be cleansed and winnowed. Then will appear the wheat which lay amidst the chaff. Do you wish to discover the good at present? Be good yourself."* Many monastic institutions arose in the middle ages, and effectually fostered piety and such learning as the circumstances of the times admitted. From earliest youth during a long life many preserved their innocence, under the shelter of the cloister. Others went forth from it, with the zeal of the Baptist, to confront a corrupt world, and to announce the judgments of God against the impenitent. It was in them that St. Bernard, St. Peter Damiani, St. Gregory VII., with many other eminent saints, were trained and prepared for vindicating the integrity of faith and the purity of morals. Others fled to the monasteries, as asylums from the prevailing corruption, or to atone by exercises of penance for the irregularities and disorders of their early life. There were also, in all the walks of life, blameless men, who lived by faith, whose conversation was in heaven, and who took occasion from the evils by which they were surrounded, to practise every sublime virtue.

* Enarr. in Ps. xlvii. 9.

Whatever may have been the scandals and abuses of the middle ages, is wholly irrelevant to the English schism, which originated manifestly and exclusively in the ungovernable passion of the monarch. As long as his own feelings were not interested, he took pride in professing his attachment to the Church, and repelled, with the applause of the Pontiff, the attack made by Luther on her sacraments. There is not the slightest evidence that he was moved in the least degree by the consideration of the disorders recorded in history, or of the examples in his own times, to break the bonds of unity. As for Cranmer, for whom you claim the praise of leader in the work of Reformation, his two successive marriages, in violation of his college obligations and priestly vows, show at once that moral considerations did not influence his career.

LETTER XIX.

On Persecution.

RIGHT REVEREND SIR:

THE proofs which Dr. Milner adduced from Tertullian, St. Leo, St. Ambrose, St. Martin, and St. Gregory the Great, that the Church disclaims the principle of persecution, have elicited from you an avowal of the fact, which, however, you limit to their times. The first instance of burning heretics alive, which you give, is in the ninth century. "This new and horrible punishment became," you say, "universal through all the countries in Europe by *established law.*" You then charge the Popes, the Bishops, and the clergy generally, with the chief influence in the enactment of the laws during the whole period of the middle ages, and especially of these laws. If you had told your readers, that Michael Curopalates, Emperor of Constantinople, was author of those executions in the ninth century, you would not have had the opportunity to charge them on the Church. The Patriarch Nicephorus opposed the imperial decree, and succeeded for a time in checking the too ardent zeal of the Emperor, observing to him that it was proper to leave room for repentance, and that ecclesiastics are not allowed to condemn to death. The Emperor Justinian II. had decreed that the Manicheans should be prosecuted, and if found guilty, burnt alive, as was done in regard to some of them. It is false that "the Church first invented the diabolical law of burning heretics." That law emanated from the civil power, which alone could inflict capital punishment. The influence of the Church was employed in the days of St. Augustin, and for ages afterwards, to prevent it. When the Circumcellions, by acts of violence and by bloodshed, had provoked the severity of the authorities, he wrote to the Proconsul of Africa, beseeching him through Jesus Christ not to punish them capitally: "We wish them to be corrected, but not put to death."*

Your chief reliance to fasten on us the principle of persecution, is the decree of the fourth Council of Lateran, held under Innocent III., in the year 1215. "We excommunicate and anathematize," say the fathers, "every heresy that raiseth itself up against this holy, orthodox, and catholic faith, which we have set forth above; condemning all heretics, by whatsoever names they may be designated, having indeed

* Ep. c. olim. cxxvii.

different faces, but their tails being joined together, since they come to the same thing through vanity." This canon is an act of the ecclesiastical authority, of an unmixed kind, and is necessarily received by all Catholics. The enactments which follow are of a different character. They are practical measures adapted to the circumstances of the times and places for which they were made: they were never generally carried out; and they have long ceased to have any force whatever. You strive hard to prove that they establish a principle which every Catholic is bound to admit, although from the very terms you must perceive, that they were directed against the pernicious errors that then threatened the destruction of society.

In the profession of faith, which is premised, the fathers declare their belief in one God, the Creator of all things, and that the devils were not from eternity, but fell by sin: they add that persons may be saved in the married state, as well as in celibacy. From this we may easily deduce the errors which were then prevailing, the same as St. Leo described, which in his time had provoked the severity of the civil authorities. "Justly did our fathers, in whose times this impious heresy burst forth, use every exertion throughout the whole world to expel the wicked frenzy from the entire Church; since even secular princes had such horror of this sacrilegious madness, that they struck the author of it, and many of his followers, with the sword of the public laws. For they saw that every regard for decorum was removed, the marriage tie dissolved, and divine and human laws subverted, if such men, professing such principles, were allowed to live anywhere. That severity was for a long time advantageous to the lenity of the Church, which, although contented with her priestly judgment, she shrinks from sanguinary revenge, is nevertheless aided by the severe enactments of Christian princes, inasmuch as those who fear corporal punishment, sometimes have recourse to the spiritual remedy."*

It is remarkable that the third Council of Lateran, held in 1179, employed this passage to explain and justify its decrees against the sectaries. The fourth Council proceeded in the same spirit, and on the same grounds, having in view their abominable practices and outrages, and accordingly directed that in case of conviction, they should be left to the bailiffs or civil officers to be punished according to law. No punishment was specified; for the confiscation of property, which is mentioned, was incidental to capital punishment, which the civil law assigned to the crime of heresy, and was only referred to probably because, by an arrangement with the authorities, the property of clergymen was excepted from the general law, and reserved to the Church

* Ep. ad Turibium.

in which they had ministered. This Council expressly forbids any clergyman to put his name to any document connected with capital punishment.

I do not, however, dissemble that the approval of these penal laws appears to be implied in this canon, especially since the authorities were required to bind themselves to extirpate all heresies branded by the Church.

A sanction also was given to the crusades against these sectaries, grounded on the necessity of protecting the defenceless, and checking those acts of violence which were constantly practised. "They practise," says the preceding Council, "such violence against Christians, as not to spare churches or monasteries, widows or orphans, aged persons or children, age or sex, but heathen-like, they destroy and devastate all things."* These outrages were countenanced and encouraged by some barons, and could not be effectually repressed, unless by a combined effort, in which volunteers from all parts should be enlisted. Hence the fathers said: "We enjoin on all the faithful for the remission of their sins, to oppose manfully such havoc, and defend with arms the Christian people."

The term *exterminare* employed in those decrees does not, in its ecclesiastical or classical acceptation, bear the same force as the correspond-

* Can. ult.

ing English word. Cicero speaks of those who forbid foreigners to reside in the cities, "*eosque exterminant*," that is, banish them beyond the city limits.* The Council uses it to express all necessary measures for breaking up and disbanding the sectarian hordes, which as armed banditti infested the country.

The various civil authorities who "claimed to be regarded as faithful," were required to cleanse their territories of "this heretical filth," under penalty of excommunication, and of forfeiting their fiefs, in case they continued a year under censure. The qualification inserted in the decree shows that it was as Catholics they were brought within its operation, and that it supposed a league between the Catholic powers to extirpate, by all just means, the prevailing sects; all agreeing to the annexing of this condition to the tenure of their fiefs. The consent of the civil powers must have been given to this arrangement, which otherwise could not take effect. There were, in fact, present there, the ambassadors of Frederick, King of Sicily, Emperor elect; of Henry, Emperor of Constantinople; of the Kings of France, England, Hungary, Jerusalem, Cyprus, Aragon; and representatives of other powers, and of various cities. It is well known, as Kent, Wheaton, and others have distinctly stated, that the councils of the

* Offic. iii. xi. post init.

middle ages bore in many respects a mixed character, so that they were in a great degree meetings of the States-General of Europe.

There is nothing to make it appear that these enactments express any Catholic principle; still less that they have any binding force at this day. If the Inquisition be in some respects conformable to them, inasmuch as the culprit is delivered over to the civil power, we must remember that it is an institution of the same age, and originally directed against the same enemies of society. Its action ceased soon after they disappeared. Its revival in Spain, at the close of the fifteenth century, was owing to political rather than religious considerations, to guard the monarchy and the nation against the secret machinations of false Christians, combined with the Moors and Jews, and its severity and cruelty, under Philip II., were occasioned by the fears of the prince, lest Spain should become the scene of wars, for religion's sake, like France and Germany. It is now extinct altogether, the Roman tribunal being merely ecclesiastical, with scarcely any civil attributions, all of which are confined to the Pontifical States. It should also be recollected that as the Inquisition was a mixed tribunal, the cognizance of the cause belonged to ecclesiastics, whose province it was to judge of what constituted heresy, whilst the punishment depended altogether on the civil power. The clergy, on committing the culprit to the civil authorities, entered a protest against blood shedding, which, although it was but a formulary, expressed, nevertheless, the reluctance of the Church to see her apostate children, by their own obstinacy in error, subjected to the highest penalty of the law. The axiom, *Ecclesia abhorret a sanguine*, "the Church abhors bloodshed," was universally acknowledged. Any clergyman concurring to the infliction of capital punishment was disqualified from exercising the ministry.

The Star Chamber, instituted under Elizabeth for the cognizance of offences against the penal laws regarding religion, consisted of forty-four commissioners, twelve of whom were bishops, many more privy councillors, and the rest either clergymen or civilians. Inquisitorial powers of the amplest kind were given to them, and any three of them were authorized to punish any word or writing tending towards heresy, schism, or sedition. All the ordinary restraints on judicial proceedings were removed, and discretionary powers granted. Elizabeth seemed to relent in this persecution of Catholics, "but such of her advisers as leaned towards the Puritan faction, and too many of the Anglican clergy, whether Puritan or not, thought no measure of charity or compassion should be extended to them."* Archbishop Parker "complained of what he called 'a Machiavel government,' that

* Strype's Whitgift, p. 212.

is, of the Queen's lenity in not absolutely rooting them out." The most secret exercise of the Catholic religion was sought out and punished. "Thus we read, in the Life of Whitgift (Archbishop of Canterbury), that on information given that some ladies and others heard mass in the house of one Edwards, by night, in the county of Denbigh, he being then Bishop of Worcester, and Vice-President of Wales, was directed to make inquiry into the facts; and finally was instructed to commit Edwards to close prison; and as for another person implicated, named Morice, if he remained obstinate, he might cause some kind of torture to be used upon him, and the like order they prayed him to use with the others." The same prelate censured a book, written about 1585, by Beale, against the Commissioners, and marked as an enormous proposition, that "he condemned, without exception of any cause, racking of grievous offenders, as being cruel, heinous, contrary to law, and unto the liberty of English subjects."

When, under James the First, it was proposed to lessen the severity of the penal laws against Catholics, the Archbishop of Canterbury remonstrated with him, assuring him that such a measure would call down upon him and upon his kingdom God's heavy anger and indignation.

If I may compare the Inquisition and Star Chamber, as Hallam, Mackintosh, and others have done, I must say that the former was far less odious. The standard by which it judged of heresy, was the doctrine of the Universal Church, believed to be infallible in her teaching; the culprits were those who had been baptized, and had acknowledged her authority, since the tribunal did not claim power over unbaptized persons, or such as had been brought up in heresy; so that its operation was confined to apostates, or to those who dissembled their heresy, in order to spread it more widely. The Star Chamber was composed of men who acknowledged no infallible authority, and whose opinions varied from those which for nearly a thousand years had prevailed in the nation. Its victims were men who, from conscientious conviction, clung to the faith of their ancestors, and without tumult or display, sought to practise the duties and enjoy the consolations of religion. In the use of the rack, both tribunals were alike, inasmuch as this mode of eliciting a confession was then adopted in all courts; in the ultimate penalty they resembled one another, although the Inquisition did not order its infliction; but in every other respect, as far as humanity, justice, and truth are concerned, the Inquisition had vastly the advantage of the Star Chamber.

You impute all the cruelty of this tribunal and of the laws made under Henry VIII., Edward VI., and Elizabeth, to the principles of Popery, which the reformers had not yet unlearned, of which you find evidence in the statute for the burning of heretics, "de hæretico comburendo," passed in the fifteenth century, in conformity, as you allege, with the canon of Lateran. As the Reformers professed no respect for the principles of the Church, and boasted of extraordinary light in the work which they had undertaken, we should have expected them to have soon rid themselves of any prejudice so repugnant to humanity. The statute alluded to was enacted in the year 1400, nearly two centuries after the Council of Lateran, and without any reference to its canons. The civil law, long before that Council, attached the penalty of death to heresy, and the English statute was passed conformably to that general jurisprudence, when the Lollards, by riots and insurrection, awakened the fears of the government. To the honor of England it must be said, that very few instances occurred of punishment on the score of religion, up to the time of Henry VIII. The principle on which the English courts proceeded, is stated by the late Chief Justice of Delaware, Thomas Clayton, in justification of his judgment in a case of most revolting blasphemy, to which he attached an extremely mild penalty: "Infidelity is proved by all history to be in character not less intolerant than fanaticism. In all cases where the tendency of any man's acts or words was, in the judgment of a common law court, to disturb the common peace of the land, of which it was the preserver and protector, or to lead to a breach of it, and the good order of society, considered merely as a civil institution, the common law avenged the wrong done to civil society alone. He, therefore, who subverted, reviled, or ridiculed the religion of our English ancestors, was punished at common law, not for his offence against his God, but for his offence against man, whose peace and safety, as they believed, was endangered by such conduct. . . . . . To sustain the soundness of this opinion, their descendants point us to the tears and blood of revolutionary France during that reign of terror, when infidelity triumphed, and the abrogation of the Christian faith was succeeded by the worship of the goddess of reason, and they aver that WITHOUT THIS RELIGION, NO NATION HAS EVER YET CONTINUED FREE."*

The same principle was doubtless common to the legislators and courts of other Catholic nations, although from the usual connection of violence with heresy, the mere profession of it came to be regarded as a crime punishable by the civil authority. Catholic jurists and divines supported this legislation, and the Reformers, Calvin, Beza, and many others, expressly maintained it, with this difference, that they limited its application to those who, like Servetus, denied the leading mysteries of faith, or extended it to

* State vs. Chandler, 2 Harrington, Delaware, p. 557.

those who clung to the ancient religion. The punishment of Jerom of Prague, and John Huss, with which you reproach us, was not for innoxious errors, but for tenets which sapped the foundations of society, by making obedience dependent on the moral integrity of the ruler. It was not in violation of the safe conduct granted to them, which was in general terms to secure them from molestation, that they might present themselves for trial, without defeating the ends of justice. It was not the act of the Council, which expressly declared that its power did not extend beyond the sentence of excommunication.* It is untrue, then, that, as you assert, "the fathers had the satisfaction of committing them to the flames." In regard to all that has been done at any time according to legal process, it is fair to examine the nature of the errors professed, and the actions of the sectaries themselves, before we pronounce judgment. St. Augustin, when reproached by the Donatists with the persecuting laws enforced against them, replied: "If any severity inconsistent with Christian lenity has, at any time, been exercised towards them, it displeases all true Christians;"† and although he defended the laws as rendered necessary by their outrages, he deprecated the infliction of capital punishment: "No good man

* Sess. xv. See Labbe's Conc. t. xii. p. 129.

† L. 1 contra ep. Parmen. c. xiii.

in the Catholic Church approves of the capital punishment of a heretic."* If, in after ages, ecclesiastics have defended such enactments, it has been in consequence of the peculiar atrocities which accompanied the profession of heresy. As to treachery, assassination, and massacre, words cannot express our horror for those crimes, by whomsoever they may be committed. The massacre of St. Bartholomew was the unpremeditated act of Charles IX., instigated by his mother, Catharine, under the apprehension of a conspiracy against the royal family, as well as religion.† The rejoicings at Rome arose from the false representations of the French ambassador, who stated that by an act of summary justice, the machinations of the rebels had been frustrated. The crimes which they had already perpetrated, the assassinations, revolts, and sacrileges of which they had been guilty, prepared men to believe the evil designs which were imputed to them. In like manner the assassinations ordered by Henry III., and the countenance given by him to the enemies of religion, caused his own assassination to be regarded as a just visitation of Providence, although the treachery by which he fell deserved all execration. Cardinal Gotti maintains that Clement,

* Contra Crescon. l. iii. c. 4, n. 55.

† See vindication of certain passages in the fourth and fifth volumes of the History of England, by J. Lingard, D.D.

his reputed murderer, had no share in his death, but was himself a victim of the conspiracy by which the monarch fell.*

The executions under Queen Mary, had no reference whatever to the canons of Lateran, as you allege. Mary, herself, was humane and disposed to be tolerant, until the treasonable conduct of the Reformers led to the adoption of severe counsels. When she first came to the throne, she assured the lord mayor and the aldermen of London, that "she meant graciously not to compel or strain other people's consciences." This forbearance was soon abused; preachers publicly styled her Jezabel; a priest, celebrating Mass in the Church of St. Bartholomew, in Smithfield, was insulted;† a preacher at St. Paul's Cross was hooted at, and narrowly escaped with his life, a dagger being flung at his head;‡ "as a priest was administering the eucharist in St. Margaret's Church, Westminster, a man drew a hanger, and wounded him upon the head, hand, and other parts of his body;"§ a conspiracy was formed, of which Sir Thomas Wyatt was leader, and to which Poinet, Protestant Bishop of Winchester, was a party, to dethrone the Queen, and restore the Protestant ascendency. Another conspiracy of the like nature was afterwards entered into. To these

* Vera Ecclesia Christi, c. iii. § 3. † Soames, iv. p. 31.
‡ Strype, Eccl. Mem. iv. p. 33; Heylin, Hist. Ref. p. 22.
§ Soames iv. p. 403. Strype, Eccl. Mem. iii. p. 210–212.

lawless and treasonable proceedings we must ascribe her change of policy. The two hundred and eighty-eight executions of sectaries, which are reported to have taken place during the last four years of her reign, are reduced to two hundred by Dr. Lingard, who regards the others as cases of treason. The Catholic prelates, generally, especially Cardinal Pole, were averse to these sanguinary measures: "He said, pastors ought to have bowels, even to their straying sheep; bishops were fathers, and ought to look on those that erred as their sick children, and not for that to kill them."* Alphonsus di Castro, a Spanish friar, the chaplain of Philip, "in a sermon before that monarch, preached largely against the taking away of the people's lives for religion—and hereupon there was a stop for several weeks to these severities."† "The bishops," says Soames, "eagerly availed themselves of any subterfuge, whereby they could escape pronouncing these revolting sentences."‡ They could not decline the office enjoined on them by law to try culprits arraigned for heresy, and they were bound to deliver them when convicted to the secular power, with a recommendation to mercy. Bonner, Bishop of London, wrote: "I marvel that other men will trouble me with their matters, but I must be

* Burnet ii. p. 467.

† Ib. p. 477.

‡ Hist. Ref. iv. p. 412.

obedient to my betters, and I fear men speak of me otherwise than I deserve."* All Catholics at this day deplore these executions, which can only be ascribed to mistaken state policy, adopted under great provocation. No principle of the Catholic religion dictated it.

When you charge the Jesuit missionaries in the Indies with cruelty and persecution, you mistake entirely their character. Indulgence and kindness have always distinguished them in their labors, whether to convert the heathen, or to reclaim sinners; so that the charges against them always turned on their extreme condescension, as you may judge from what you state of their toleration of Chinese usages. They have never been connected with the Inquisition, and never advocated measures of severity towards sectaries. If in Goa cruelty was practised at any time, the Portuguese authorities should bear the censure. You equally mistake Catholic principles, when you assert that "our religion makes it a duty to torture and burn all dissenters for the love of God." The direct contrary is the truth. Our religion teaches us to love all mankind, to bear with their errors and vices, to forgive the wrongs which they do to us, and to return them by blessings. We know the spirit of Him who was meek and humble of heart. When you justify the men who shed the blood of our peaceful missionaries, and vir-

* Foxe, iii. p. 462; vol. ii. p. 29.

tually instigate others to sacrifice us "as the worst enemies of mankind;" when you call our martyrs "martyrs of the devil,"* we pity your ignorance of our real principles, and pardon your impiety. To you, who are wont to speak plainly, I need not apologize for this language.

You boast that the Church of England never persecuted. I am at a loss to know what I am to understand by that church. If the legal heads of it, and the authors and promoters of the schism be considered, Henry VIII. and Elizabeth were certainly persecutors of the worst kind. Edward VI. was so misled by his tutors that he strove to force his own sister to abjure her faith. Cranmer, for whom you claim the great merit of spreading the new principles, concurred with Somerset, the Protector, in procuring the enactment of most sanguinary laws against the professors of the ancient creed. "All who should deny the king's supremacy were for the first offence to forfeit their goods and chattels, and to suffer imprisonment during pleasure; for the second, they were to incur the penalties of *præmunire;* for the third, they were to be attainted as traitors."† From its first existence as the creature of Royalty, it had no power of action, no independent voice, it could only speak or act through the Parliament, or the sovereign; consequently those Acts which passed

* Vol. ii. p. 29.

† Soames, iii. p. 185.

without opposition from its prelates, and still more those which were suggested and supported by them, such as the Acts under Edward, which generally received the warm support of Cranmer, may be fairly taken for their own. In the book of ecclesiastical laws, which he composed by order of Edward, the penalty of death, with confiscation of goods, is denounced against all who deny the Catholic faith, by which the mystery of the Trinity seems there specially meant. Persons accused of heresy—which was a more comprehensive term—were to be imprisoned, until tried, in default of security for their appearance; and if on conviction they should refuse to abjure their errors, they were to be delivered over to the secular power. The death of George Van Parr, a Hollander resident in London, found guilty of Arianism, is justly laid to Cranmer's charge, as "truly the effect of those principles by which he governed himself."* When Elizabeth came to the throne, an Act of Parliament was passed, declaring her "supream governesse"† of the Church of England, which every ecclesiastical person was required to acknowledge on oath, under penalty of forfeiture of his benefice; followed by another Act, which decreed, that if "any should either by discourse or in writing, set forth the authority of any foreign power, or do anything for the ad-

* Burnet, ii. p. 181.

† Heylin, p. 108.

vancement of it, they were for the first offence to forfeit all their goods and chattels; and if they had not goods to the value of twenty pounds, they were to be imprisoned a whole year; and for the second offence, they were to incur the pains of a *præmunire;* and the third offence was treason."* This gentle means was employed to enforce the claims of the Supreme Governess of the Church of England! All the bishops, except Kitchen of Landaff, fourteen or fifteen in number, refusing to take the oath of supremacy, were deprived of their sees and committed to prison. Cranmer, Parker, Whitgift, and Bancroft, all occupants of Canterbury, advocated the persecution of Catholics. The Convocation, in 1577, ordered Roland Jenks, a Catholic bookseller in Oxford, to be apprehended for speaking against the new religion, put in irons, his goods seized, and his trial to take place at the ensuing assizes; when he was sentenced to have his ears nailed to the pillory, and to set himself free by cutting them off with his own hand. The Church by law established, was forced on a reluctant people by penal laws, devised with ingenuity, and executed without mercy. Its rise and progress are written in the blood of the professors of the ancient faith; and at every attempt to loose the chains of its victims, the hellish yell was raised to prevent their relief,

* Burnet, iii. p. 602.

"The Church is in danger!" "I cannot conceive," said Edmund Burke—insinuating the truth of the charge, whilst he affected to repel it—"how anything worse can be said of the Protestant religion of the Church of England than this, that wherever it is judged proper to give it a legal establishment, it becomes necessary to deprive the body of the people, if they adhere to their old opinions, of 'their liberties and of all their free customs,' and to reduce them to a state of civil servitude."*

Some instances may be necessary to illustrate the working of this penal system. Sir Edward Waldgrave and his Lady, in 1561, were sent to the Tower, for hearing Mass, and having a priest in their house, and many others were punished in like manner. Two bishops, in 1562, wrote to the Council advising that a priest, found in Lady Carew's house, be put to some kind of torment, to elicit a confession that might enable the Queen to levy great fines for violation of the law by the Catholic worship.† In the year 1563, the obligation of taking the oath of supremacy was extended to the whole Catholic population. The refusal to take it was punishable with forfeiture and imprisonment, and a second refusal, when tendered anew, after three months, subjected the recusant to the penalties of high

* Letter to Sir Hercules Langrishe, M. P.

† Hallam, Constit. Hist. i. p. 153.

treason.* In vain did Lord Montague plead: "I do entreat whether it be just to make this penal statute to force the subjects of this realm to receive and believe the religion of Protestants on pain of death." Hallam observes: "In Strype's collections, we find abundance of persons harassed for recusancy; that is, for not attending the Protestant Church, and driven to insincere promises of conformity. Others were dragged before the ecclesiastical commission for harboring priests." "By stealth, at the dead of night, in private chambers, in the secret lurking places of an ill-peopled country, with all the mystery that subdues the imagination, with all the mutual trust that invigorates constancy, these proscribed ecclesiastics celebrated their solemn rites, more impressive in such concealment, than if surrounded by all their former splendor."*

You admit that "the laws passed in the reign of Elizabeth, were exceedingly severe," and add: "but the alarms and acts of Rome made them necessary, in self-protection."‡ Now it is certain that Elizabeth had been acknowledged Queen with acclamation by her Catholic subjects, and had no cause of dissatisfaction with them during the first ten years of her reign, during which these sanguinary enactments were

* Hallam, Const. Hist. i. p. 161, 163.

† V. Eliz. c. i.

‡ Vol. ii. p. 388.

made. You allege that she had been excommunicated by the Pope. The Bull is dated 25th February, 1570, and cannot, therefore, have been the cause of enactments made so far back as 1559. These, followed by the process against Mary Stuart, gave occasion to the excommunication. Even afterwards, the Catholics generally continued to give undoubted proofs of their loyalty, although extreme persecution maddened some into revolt.

The chief victims under Elizabeth were sacrificed for their religion, without a shadow of other offence against the laws. Edward Hanse, formerly a Protestant clergyman, afterwards a priest, was executed, for acknowledging that the Pope had then the same authority in England that he had a hundred years before. Campion, a convert likewise, and a Jesuit, after having endured the rack many times, was convicted of treason, although he solemnly acknowledged Elizabeth as Queen. Mackintosh and Hallam acknowledge that the charge was groundless. He, with Sherwin and Briant, suffered the death of traitors. Six others, after long imprisonment, were executed on 30th May, 1582.

"The rack seldom stood idle in the Tower for all the latter part of Elizabeth's reign."* *The scavenger's daughter*, or *hoop*, was another instrument of torture, in which the body was com-

* Hallam, Const. Hist. i. p. 200.

pressed until the head and feet met. I shall not undertake to describe the other instruments of torture, or the cruelties practised towards individuals.

The offences for which Catholics suffered were generally religious exercises. Cuthbert Mayne, a priest in Cornwall, charged with having obtained a Bull from Rome, (no other than the copy of a Bull of Jubilee,) of denying the supremacy, and of saying Mass, was convicted on mere presumptions, and hanged, "without any charge against him but his religion."* Tregian, in whose house Mayne had celebrated Mass, lingered in prison eight-and-twenty years. Two other priests suffered at Tyburn for the same offence.

In the year 1585, thirteen clergymen, four laymen, and a lady named Cithero, suffered the death of traitors, merely for their religion. She was found guilty of harboring priests. I forbear narrating the barbarous manner of her execution. In 1586, Mrs. Ward was hanged, drawn and quartered, for assisting a priest to escape; in 1601, Mrs. Lyne was punished in like manner, for the same offence. In 1587, eight Catholics were executed; in 1588, nearly forty, the majority of whom were priests. "The Catholic martyrs, under Elizabeth," says Hallam, "amount

* Hallam, Const. Hist. i. p. 196; see also Mackintosh, iii. p. 284; Bridgewater, p. 34, 35; Stowe, an. 1577.

to no inconsiderable number. Dodd reckons them at 191; Milner has raised the list to 204. Fifteen of these, according to him, suffered for denying the Queen's supremacy, 126 for exercising their ministry, and the rest for being reconciled to the Romish Church. Many others died of hardships in prison, and many were deprived of their property."* The heavy fines constantly levied for not attending at the new service, the imprisonment of multitudes for this offence, and the punishment of many, show the most unrelenting persecution, on the largest scale possible. Some of them had their ears bored with a hot iron, others were publicly whipped.

Your plea of necessity for these persecutions, is by anticipation rejected by Hallam. "The statutes of Elizabeth's reign, comprehend every one of these progressive degrees of restraint and persecution. And it is much to be regretted that any writers worthy of respect should, either through undue prejudice against an adverse religion, or through timid acquiescence in whatever has been enacted, have offered for this odious code the false pretext of political necessity."†

I should never end were I to enter into a detail of the persecutions endured by the Catholics of Ireland, for adherence to the ancient

* Vol. i. p. 221. † Ibid. p. 229.

faith. There, as well as in England, attendance at the reformed worship was compulsory, and the celebration of Mass, or the being present at it, exposed priest and people to heavy punishment, even to the penalties of high treason. To employ a Catholic teacher was rigorously forbidden, and to send one's children abroad for education, was a heinous offence, subjecting the parent to loss of property, the child, if he did not return within a limited time, to outlawry, forfeiture of estate, and other severe penalties. An apostate son could drive his aged parents, and his brothers and sisters, from their home. These are among the least of the grievances which pressed down to the earth our faithful ancestors. All this has passed away. To whom should we be grateful? Not surely to the Church of England or of Ireland, whose prelates, with some rare exception, such as Bathurst of Norwich, and Watson of Landaff, steadily and strenuously to the last moment supported the penal laws. Your own sentiments and dispositions are not questionable. You assert that "England could not exercise her Christian liberty, nor hope to preserve it, if she did not regard the Pope as the enemy of the State, as well as of the Church."* This is, doubtless, intended as a hint to those, who, under the pretext of opposing foreigners, are laboring to dis-

* Vol. ii. p. 389.

franchise Catholics, in this land of freedom, and accordingly you, although yourself of foreign birth, have appeared in their ranks, stimulating them in the career of intolerance.

In the United States, at least, Catholics are without reproach on this head. The colony of Maryland, founded by a nobleman of our communion, gave the first example of freedom of conscience to an extent at that time considerable, namely, for all who professed to believe in our Lord Jesus Christ. Since the achievement of our national independence, we have never manifested the slightest disposition to disturb the harmony which was provided for by guaranteeing to all equal rights, irrespective of religious differences. In all the relations of life, we have shown practical liberality and charity, without compromising any principle of our religion. Yet you would proscribe us, "because," to borrow the language of Edmund Burke, "in contradiction to experience and common sense, you think proper to imagine that our principles are subversive of common human society."* If the example of Massachusetts, which has just now declared us ineligible to office, be followed by other States, and the great principle, which has hitherto been our boast as a nation, that conscience should be free, be abandoned, it requires no prophet to foretel that

* Letter to Sir Hercules Langrishe, M. P.

the various sects which now combine to proscribe us, will contend among themselves for the mastery, and that dissensions and strife will succeed the peace and harmony which our social relations have hitherto presented. I venture not to look further into futurity, lest I be a prophet of evil; but I am consoled by the reflection that if the grand fabric of our liberties be shaken by any civil convulsion, Catholics will, at least, be guiltless of having contributed, even in a remote degree, to the catastrophe.

LETTER XX.

On Henry VIII.

RIGHT REVEREND SIR:

YOU have become, to a great extent, the apologist of Henry VIII.; but never did you undertake a cause more desperate. You labor to show that he acted from scruples of conscience in regard to the validity of his marriage with Catherine; and in disregard of all history, you maintain that his passion for Anne Boleyn was not the cause of his revolt against the authority of the Holy See. It is scarcely necessary to enter into the details by which you endeavor to support your first position, since, as Sir James Mackintosh writes, no trace can be found of such scruples before the year 1527, when the parties had been more than seventeen years united in wedlock.* If, at this day, you yourself were consulted as to the existence of any divine law, obligatory on Christians, forbidding marriage with the wife of a deceased

* History of England, p. 149.

brother, I presume you would not hesitate to give a negative reply. Such marriages are frequent among the various sects, and are contracted occasionally even by ministers. The law of Leviticus regarded the Jews only, and was limited by the exception of the case of a brother dying without issue. The scruples of Henry were simultaneous with his affection for Anne Boleyn, according to the same historian; and his whole conduct in pursuit of the divorce was, as Tytler avows, "marked by hypocrisy, selfishness, and a fixed determination to gratify his passions."* The artifices employed to obtain a favorable answer from the Universities, are well known; and the bribes which were lavished, are matters of record.†

You infer from the fact that Josephine was set aside by Napoleon, that Catherine might have been discarded by Henry, without forfeiture of the communion of the Church; and you discover no difference in the cases, unless that the rights of Catherine were supported by her nephew Charles V., whilst Josephine stood unprotected. Yet the marriage of Josephine had taken place irregularly, in times of confusion and disorder, which occasioned strong doubts of its validity. That of Catherine was celebrated with solemnity by the express au-

* Life of Henry VIII. p. 242.

† See Burnet, 1 Rec. 2, xxxviii.; Strype, App. vol. v. pp. 476–479.

thority of the Church. Besides, the Pope never sanctioned the divorce of Josephine, which he could not effectually oppose at the time at which it was declared. It is unnecessary to inquire how far Clement may have been influenced by the fear of Charles V. It is known that he cherished special affection for Henry; and if he did not yield to his importunity, it is fair to ascribe it to those considerations of justice and right which become the chief Bishop of the Church. You contend that he, in fact, did yield, and that he authorized Henry to marry any other woman whom he pleased, even although the relationship should be like that on which the plea for divorce was grounded, provided it were not the same precisely; but you mistake a conditional dispensation, which was to take effect only in the contingency of the divorce being pronounced by the legate, after cognizance of the cause, for an absolute and unqualified concession. The envoys of Henry presented to Clement, at Orvieto, two documents for his signature, which, with some reluctance, he attached to them; one of them, empowering Wolsey as legate to hear the case, the other dispensing Henry, if the result were in his favor, from other impediments which were believed to exist in respect to Anne. Clement also was reported to have said, that if Henry felt assured that his marriage with Catherine was null, his shortest way to bring the matter to an issue, was to marry another woman, and then let the validity of this second contract be tried. This may have been no more than an intimation, that the Pope did not believe him to be sincere. Heylin, your own historian, says: "This king being violently hurried with the transport of some private affections, and finding that the Pope appeared the greatest obstacle to his desires, he first divested him by degrees of that supremacy which had been challenged and enjoyed by his predecessors for some ages past, and finally extinguished his authority in the realm of England."* Burnet concurs in this view: "When Henry began his reformation, his design seemed to have been, in the whole progress of these changes, to terrify the Court of Rome, and force the Pope into a compliance with what he desired."†

You argue that the separation was not caused by the refusal of Clement to grant the divorce, since it took place before the adverse decision was known in England. It is true that when the Act of Parliament which separated England from the Holy See, received the Royal assent, the final judgment had not been reported; but it was already anticipated, and all hope of success had vanished. On the 20th March, 1534, the Act passed; on 23d March, sentence was pronounced at Rome. Despair drove the dis-

* Preface to History of the Reformation. † Preface, vol. i.

appointed suitor to retaliate by acts of insubordination and revolt.

You represent all the English bishops but Fisher, and all the distinguished laymen except More, as favorable to the divorce, but history attests the contrary. Cardinal Wolsey himself, who lent his services to have the matter canvassed, and promoted, if the case admitted it, was never satisfied as to its lawfulness, and often employed remonstrance to dissuade the prince from the prosecution of his design, as on his death-bed he assured Kyngston, "I do assure you I have often kneeled before him, sometimes for three hours together, to persuade him from his appetite, and could not prevail."* His disgrace was brought on by his determination to judge justly, without regard to the royal inclination. The University of Cambridge was opposed to it, although by great management a favorable answer was obtained, clogged, however, with a condition which was thought to vitiate it altogether.† Of Oxford, Tytler says, that "the decision could not be considered as altogether unbiassed and impartial."‡ The Bishop of Bayonne states "that few of their divines could be induced to pronounce in favor of the King."§ The sense of the nation was evidently against the divorce, and the people hesitated not to declare, that whosoever should marry the Princess

* Cavendish, p. 535. † Burnet, 1 Rec. xxxii. pp. 125, 127.
‡ Tytler, p. 299. § Apud Le Grand, iii. 205.

Mary, Catherine's daughter, would become the rightful King of England on the demise of Henry; the nobles, says Le Grand, thought the same, if they were silent on the subject.* Cardinal Pole writes to Henry: "In the beginning, your cause, together with all its patrons, was exploded in all the schools of your own kingdom."† Soames states that "the clergy had become obnoxious to the King, because they were generally unfavorable to his divorce."‡

Sir Henry Spelman does not hesitate to ascribe the determination of Henry to a penal judgment. "Like Saul, forsaken of God, he falls from one sin to another. Queen Catherine (the wife of his bosom for twenty years), must now be put away, the marriage declared void."§ That he should have found men to pander to his passion, by maintaining the invalidity of the marriage, is not a matter of surprise; that others in greater number withheld the expression of their opposition, may be easily imagined; but there is not a shadow of proof for asserting that the free and unbiassed judgment of the clergy, sustained him in his effort to loose the sacred tie.

You say that "no earthly policy can possibly account for Henry's course. It was the work of Divine Providence, who raised up this man of energy and passion to prepare the way for the

* Thompson's Memoirs, vol. ii. p. 91. † F. lxxvii.
‡ Vol. i. p. 279. § *De non temerandis ecclesiis.* Preface.

restoration of His truth, in mercy to mankind."* Every historian, Protestant as well as Catholic, has pointed out the policy which led this prince step by step to the fatal gulf. His passion for Anne Boleyn was the spring of the whole movement. As long as he cherished hope of obtaining the sanction of the Pope for abandoning Catherine, he did not think of resisting his authority; but finding himself baffled, he had recourse to intimidation. Acting under the advice of Thomas Cromwell, by the disgrace of Wolsey, and the penalties of the statute of provisors, he terrified the clergy into an acknowledgment of his new title of "Protector and Supreme Head of the Church of England," qualified, however, by them, in order to reconcile their consciences to its admission, by the clause, "as far as the law of Christ will allow." Tytler records the opposition and protests of several prelates, when Henry insisted on the omission of this qualification. Tunstal, Bishop of Durham, procured a Bull of translation from Rome, without being prosecuted according to statute—"a proof that the King's mind was yet in a state of irresolution, and that probably, at this moment, his purpose was rather to intimidate, than absolutely to separate from the Roman See."† Even when, in January, 1532, the payment of annates was forbidden, "a clause in the Act gave it the air of intimidation. It was enacted that the King be

* Vol. i. p. 52. † Tytler, p. 313.

empowered, at any time before Easter, 1533, or before the next session of Parliament, to declare, by letters patent, whether any, or what of the provisions of this Act should be carried into effect. None who considered this clause, could doubt that the King's principal object in procuring its insertion, was to overawe the Court of Rome by means of the discretionary power left in his hands."* In January, 1533, another Act was passed, declaring the King supreme head of the Church of England, but containing a proviso "which suspended its execution till midsummer, and enabled the King on or before that day to repeal it; probably adopted with some remaining hope that it might have terrors enough to countervail those which were inspired by the imperial armies."† Mackintosh imagined that fear, rather than a sense of duty, swayed the councils of the Pontiff. Henry, according to the testimony of Gardiner, twice seriously thought of returning to unity; but these visitations of grace were resisted, and the unhappy man, whose work against Luther obtained from Leo X. the title of "Defender of the Faith," which is still borne by the Sovereign, died out of the communion of the Church, having to answer to God for one of the worst schisms that ever tried the strength of this Divine institution. I agree with you that Divine Providence raised

* Soames's Hist. of Reform, vol. i. pp. 290, 295.

† Mackintosh's Hist. of England, vol. ii. p. 174.

him up; but only as it raised up Pharao, to show to the world how powerless are the machinations of Princes against the counsels of God.

With apparent complacency you state that Bishop Fisher and Chancellor More suffered as traitors. If you had explained wherein their treason consisted, your readers would have been better able to judge of their titles to respect and veneration. Fisher, who was eighty years of age, during his whole life had been devoted to religion, and distinguished by his attachment to his sovereigns, Henry VII., whose councillor he had been, and his son, the eighth Henry. His learning was a source of pride to the monarch, who adopted as his own work the defence of the Seven Sacraments against Luther, which is thought to have been the production of Fisher's pen. He had never faltered in his allegiance. When accused for not having disclosed the visionary dreams of Catharine Barton, who had foretold the King's death, he gave a satisfactory excuse, that he knew that the King was aware of them from other sources. Yet on this pretext he was found guilty of misprision of treason, despoiled of his estate, and sentenced to imprisonment. When he had escaped the storm by a sacrifice of three hundred pounds, he was called on to swear to support the succession, as regulated by a special Act passed by order of Henry, which he freely consented to do; but the oath presented to him contained a declaration of the invalidity of Henry's first marriage, and the validity of the second, as also a disclaimer of all foreign authority, even spiritual, in the realm of England. To this his conscience was invincibly opposed, and for no other crime the hoary prelate was cast into a dungeon, and left to languish there with scarcely the necessary support of life, for above a year, thence to be dragged to the scaffold, and perish *as a traitor.* He died, however, with the serenity, fortitude, and joy of a martyr, having dressed as for a festival, and answered his servant, who expressed surprise at his care in dressing: "Dost thou not know that this is my wedding day?" At his last moments he declared most truly that he died for the faith of Christ's Holy Catholic Church. Soames says: "Bishop Fisher is a martyr to their cause, of whom the Roman Catholics have good reason to be proud."* Mackintosh describes him as "a pious minister, of extreme simplicity of life, and sweetness of temper, and as an indefatigable and enthusiastic restorer of learning, worthy to be had in all honorable remembrance."†

Sir Thomas More, whom also you are pleased to class with traitors, was guilty of no greater crime than the venerable Bishop of Rochester. He had cautiously abstained from uttering anything disrespectful to his Sovereign, but faithfully resisted every effort to induce him to take the obnoxious oath. After lingering in prison for a

* Vol. ii. pp. 32, 36.

† Vol. ii. pp. 177, 179.

year, he was brought to trial on the charge of treason, pursuant to an Act recently passed which created a new kind of treason, that of doing anything by writing or act which was to the slander, disturbance or prejudice of the marriage with the Lady Anne. The amount of the testimony given by a law officer of the crown, who had visited him in prison, with a view to elicit some expression which might serve for his condemnation, was, that "the statute was a two-edged sword; for if he spoke against it, he should be the cause of the death of his body; and if he assented to it, he should purchase the death of his soul." On this ground he was found guilty, and suffered as a traitor, although *by special favor*, beheading was substituted for the ordinary punishment. Thus perished the first lay Chancellor of England, a man of great learning, sweet manners, eminent piety, and unfaltering devotion to his Sovereign, in all things consistent with the Divine law. Cheerfully, joyfully, he met death. The butchery of these two eminent men marks Henry as one of the most infamous and cruel tyrants who ever abused the sovereign power. The English schism, of which he was the author, was begun in lust, and cemented in blood. To pretend that it was provoked by excesses on the part of the Church, or that it was directed to restore the primitive order of church government, or that it was accomplished by the free action of the ecclesiastical authorities of England, is to falsify all history. Its rise and progress are plainly traced to the worst of human passions.

You had better utterly abandon the defence of a monster, in whom lust and cruelty struggled for the ascendency. The unfortunate Anne Boleyn soon experienced his vengeance, when Jane Seymour had won his affection. On the day of her execution he dressed in white, went a hunting, and the next day took Jane to his bed as a wedded wife. He afterwards put aside Anne of Cleves, who was accused of no crime, and ordered Catharine Howard, another of his wives, to the scaffold. Truly did Sir James Mackintosh say, that "Henry approached as nearly to the ideal of perfect wickedness as the infirmities of human nature will allow."* Sir Henry Spelman, after enumerating his wives, says: "Here's wives enough. to have peopled another Canaan, had he had Jacob's blessing; but his three last are childless, and the children of the two first are, by statute, declared illegitimate, and not inheritable to the crown." "They all successively sway his sceptre, and all die childless, and his family is extinct, and like Herostratus, his name not mentioned but with his crimes."†

The persecutions carried on by Henry VIII., and his abettors, were not directed against the

* Vol. ii. p. 204. † De non temerandis ecclesiis. Preface.

enemies of order and society, but against unoffending men, whose only crime was their adherence to the ancient faith. Three Carthusian priors, a monk of Sion, and two others, one of whom was a secular priest, were charged with high treason, and through the violence and threats of Thomas Cromwell, found guilty by a reluctant jury, who avowed their unwillingness to give such a verdict. Prior Houghton, at the place of execution, declared his entire devotion to the King, but that he feared God, whom he should offend by abjuring the doctrine of the Church. They were all, nevertheless, hung, cut down before death, disembowelled and quartered in the most shocking manner. In expiring, Houghton cried: "Most holy Lord Jesus, have mercy upon me in this hour." "Whilst in prison they were horribly tortured, being each fastened to an upright post by means of iron chains drawn tight round their necks and thighs, without being once loosened during the whole fortnight of their imprisonment."* Three other Carthusians, for refusing to take the oath of Supremacy, were executed soon after. Nine or ten more were put in such close confinement, that they all died but one, who was executed. Two Carthusians, at York, were put to death for the same cause. Fifty Franciscans perished from the rigor of their imprisonment, the rest were banished. Fourteen Catholics suffered

* Waterworth, Lecture ii. on the Reformation, note. He cites Strype, Eccles. Mem. vol. i. p. 314.

subsequently for denying the King's supremacy in ecclesiastical concerns, whilst ten Protestants were also sent to the stake. On one occasion, "to exhibit his impartiality, as head of the Church, the King commanded them to be placed together in pairs, Catholic and Lutheran, on the same hurdle, and thus dragged from the Tower to Smithfield, where the assertors of the Papal authority were hanged as traitors, and their companions consumed at the stake as heretics."*

In extenuation of the cruelty of Henry, you say, "it was a small matter in comparison with the tortures and death inflicted by your old Inquisition, and universally sanctioned throughout Europe, previous to the Reformation." I know of no atrocity to equal it. The Inquisition saved from death the penitent heretic twice, and if in the third instance it delivered the convict to the civil authorities, it was because its power of pardon was limited. The standard of its judgments was not the caprice of any individual potentate or ecclesiastic, but the faith of the Universal Church. Henry inflicted death on peaceable men, who retained the faith which he himself professed, because they would not recognize in him a supremacy in things spiritual, which had never been claimed by any of his predecessors. You assert that it was "the same

* Tytler, p. 428.

supremacy which was exercised by the Christian emperors for more than ten centuries."* What power the Arian Emperors may have claimed or exercised, I care not; but it is certain that Catholic princes acknowledged that they had no power in things spiritual, professing themselves obedient children of the Church, and deeming it a duty and a privilege to support her decrees by their authority. St. Ambrose praises Constantine for not interfering in the case of two bishops of Mœsia (Bulgaria), which he referred to their colleagues in the episcopate: "He would not wrong the priests; he appointed the bishops themselves to be the judges."† The celebrated Osius, Bishop of Corduba, nobly resisted the attempt of the Arian Emperor Constantius, to dictate to the bishops. "Do not meddle with church affairs, or send us mandates in regard to them, but be content to learn from us. God has given you the empire. He has charged us with the interests of the Church."‡ Certainly no Catholic King claimed the title or power ascribed to Henry in the Act of Parliament, which recognizing him as "supreme head on earth of the Church of England," granted him "full power to correct and amend any errors, heresies, abuses, &c., which, by any manner ecclesiastical jurisdiction might be reformed or redressed."§

* Vol. i. 37. † Conc. Aquil. col. 826, tom. i. col. Hard.

‡ Apud Athanas. Ep. ad solit. vitam agentes.

§ Mackintosh Hist. of Eng. vol. ii. p. 175.

The savage cruelty of the monster appeared particularly in his sending to the scaffold his nearest female relative, the Countess of Salisbury, in her seventieth year, accused of no crime whatever, merely to avenge himself of her son, Cardinal Pole, who had incurred his displeasure by accepting promotion in the Roman Court.

You labor to show that neither the prince, nor his abettors, had need of having recourse to violent measures for acquiring the property of the various Orders, since even Wolsey had been authorized to suppress forty small monasteries, for the execution of a favorite project, the endowment of two colleges. But what Pope would authorize the wanton and general plunder of all the monasteries? Sir William Dugdale is an unexceptionable witness, that reform was only a pretext for spoliation, in order to enrich the coffers of the King and of his accomplices: "It was not the strict and regular lives, or anything that may be said in behalf of the monasteries, that could prevent their ruin thus approaching. So great an aim had the King to make himself thereby glorious, and many others no less hopes to be enriched in a considerable manner."* The strictest communities, whose good conduct was acknowledged by all, fell under the general ban. Among them, "the monks of the Charter-house, in the suburbs of London, were committed

* History of Warwickshire, p. 801.

to Newgate, where, with hard and barbarous usage, five of them died, and five more lay at the point of death." The Royal commissioners charged the Abbots with robbing the Church, if they presumed to secrete any of its ornaments from them. Under this pretence, "the Abbot of Glastonbury, with two of his monks, being condemned to death, was drawn from Wells upon a hurdle, then hanged upon the hill called Tor, near Glastonbury, his head set upon the Abbey gate, and his quarters disposed of to Wells, Bath, Ilchester, and Bridgewater. Nor did the Abbots of Colchester and Reading fare much better, as they that will consult the story of that time may see. And for farther terror to the rest, some priors and other ecclesiastical persons, who spake against the King's supremacy, a thing then somewhat uncouth, were condemned as traitors and executed." This is the testimony of Sir William Dugdale. The means which Henry employed to get parliamentary sanction for his rapacity, were such as we might expect. Finding that the Bill stuck in the lower house, he summoned the Commons to meet him in his gallery, where he made them wait for hours, before he made his appearance. On presenting himself, he addressed them scornfully: "I hear that my bill will not pass; but I will have it pass, or I will have some of your heads." This determined the loyal Commons to support the measure. It would be easy to swell this volume, by details of the plundering of the monasteries and churches; but it is altogether unnecessary, since the fact is notorious. Whoever will take in hand the work of Sir Henry Spelman, will see numberless proofs of it; as also awful instances of the punishment which overtook the sacrilegious plunderers. It was somewhat bold in you, sir, in the face of history, to maintain that the Reformers were influenced by no love of plunder, but by zeal for pure religion!

LETTER XXI.

On Cranmer.

RIGHT REVEREND SIR:

YOU have undertaken to be the apologist of Cranmer more decidedly than of Henry. Notwithstanding your resolution to be kind and charitable, you have penned this sentence against Dr. Milner, for presenting a most true picture of this hero of the Reformation. "The best excuse I can frame for this wanton defamer is to be found in the doctrine of that Jesuit society, of which I presume he was a member. For thus we find it laid down by some of their divines: 'It is only a venial sin, to calumniate and accuse of false crimes, in order to ruin the credit of those who speak ill of us.'"* Dr. Milner was no Jesuit, nor has this illustrious society ever held any such principles—the assertion of Pascal, the Jansenist satirist, to the contrary notwithstanding. You should pause before you speak of "those atrocious maxims of Jesuit

* Vol. i. p. 388.

morality, which Pascal so admirably exposed."* Who then is the wanton defamer? The libertinism charged on Cranmer, by Dr. Milner, is attested by every historian, and should meet no countenance from you, who are so severe on clerical delinquency. It is certain that after his priesthood, he contracted marriage secretly, or lived in concubinage with the niece of Osiander, whom he contrived to smuggle into England, and afterward sent back, when Henry, in the Six Articles, enforced sacerdotal celibacy under threat of capital punishment; but his base hypocrisy and cruelty, deserve still greater execration. He approved of the condemnation of John Fryth and Andrew Hewet to the stake, for not believing "the very corporal presence of Christ within the host and sacrament of the altar,"† which it is probable that he himself at the time disbelieved. Henry ordered him, with three other prelates, to convert or execute certain German Anabaptists, who sought to propagate their tenets. One man and woman were publicly burnt alive, besides fourteen others, who had been previously executed. His name, as well as that of Latimer, was affixed to the death-warrant of Joan Boacher and Von Parr. I am willing to pass your extravagant eulogiums of Edward VI., whose humanity or conscientiousness I honor, as manifested in his reluctance to sign the death-warrant

* Vol. ii. p. 29.

† Cranmer's Letter to Hawkins, Archeol. xviii. p. 81.

of Joan Boacher; but what must we think of Cranmer, who used all his efforts to overcome this feeling?* "Cranmer himself confessed," says Foxe, "that he had never so much to do in all his life, as to cause the King to put to his hand, saying that he would lay all the charge thereof upon Cranmer before God."† The poor youth, trained and surrounded by men of false principles, is to be pitied, rather than condemned. Can you respect Cranmer who under Henry not only concealed his own sentiments, but became his pliant agent in condemning others to the stake, for holding the same views? Can you account for his lending himself to every caprice of the monarch, even with the sacrifice of those who co-operated with him in the work of Reform? Anne Boleyn was his patron and support; yet no sooner had she incurred the displeasure of her capricious lord, than Cranmer virtually prejudged her, offering his services to the prince, and declared null, from the beginning, the marriage which he himself had sanctioned. With the same promptness, he dissolved the marriage of Henry with Anne of Cleves, for no other reason than the disgust which the prince had conceived of her. As his agent, he obtained from Catharine Howard, under a solemn promise that her life should be spared, a confession of her incontinence before

* Burnet, Ref. ii. 179.

† Foxe, 1179.

marriage; notwithstanding which she died on the scaffold, without effort on his part to obtain her pardon.

He appears to have been, in principle, a Protestant all the time; yet he accepted the office of Archbishop, and by his proctor at Rome, swore obedience to the Pope, and accepted the Articles of Catholic faith, which pledges he gave personally again at his consecration. After some demurring, he co-operated with Henry in enforcing his Six Articles, even with the penalty of death. Under Edward, he began by inculcating the Real Presence, and cautioning the people against those who denied it; as he himself did within a few months afterwards.*

You seriously undertake to justify the manifest perjury contained in the solemn profession of faith and promise of obedience, made by a man who in his heart disbelieved, and who was determined to revolt against the Papal authority. A previous protest made by him in the Chapter-house, before notaries, that he did not intend to bind himself to anything contrary to the law of God, prejudicial to the rights and prerogatives of the King, or prohibitory of such reforms in the Church of England as he might deem useful, appears to you to warrant his public act, whereby he swore, without qualification, to render obedience to the Papal mandates, and keep the

* See Soames, iii. p. 72.

Catholic faith inviolate. I must, however, state your pleas in his behalf:

First, you refer to your extracts from Fleury's Ecclesiastical History "for multiplied proofs that Cranmer was under no necessity of making such a protest at all, because the prelates of Rome had given the same construction to the oath for ages together, without any doubt or hesitation." If so, why did he make it? Truly, at all times it was understood that the obedience promised by bishops to the Pontiff was not designed to interfere with their civil allegiance, and the proviso in the oath: *salvo meo ordine—without prejudice to my rank*—might admit this interpretation. But what man of conscience could swear obedience to the spiritual authority of the chief Bishop, with the avowed intention of refusing it, in order to serve the caprice of his King, in things not appertaining to the civil order? Yet you defend this trifling with oaths by the ministers of religion.

Secondly, you "refer to the cases in which the cardinals took ground against the Popes, because in their opinion the Popes had gone astray, and the best interests of the Church required their deposition. In all such cases there was the same oath to the Pope, and it was necessary to break that oath before they could even confer about the calling of a Council." We are not now concerned with the interpretation of an oath, to determine whether extraordinary circumstances may occur, in which a departure from its letter may be justifiable; though for myself I hold to the strictest acceptation of the words; but what has this to do with the act of a man, who, at the time of taking the oath, protests in private that he does not take it in its avowed and established signification?

Thirdly, you "refer to the construction of the same oath by all the other bishops in the reign of Henry VIII., since there was not one amongst them, save Fisher, who did not go with the King against the Pope." The forced acquiescence of bishops, fearing the fâte of their martyred colleague, is no proof of the construction which they put upon their oath, much less can it justify the hypocrisy of a public oath, and a previous protest to the contrary. It is, however untrue that they acquiesced.

Fourthly, you refer to the resistance made by all the English Romanists (you mean Catholics) "against the Papal Bull of Sixtus V., in which he undertook to depose Queen Elizabeth." All these examples are most unhappily chosen, as they afford no parallel to the case. The English Catholics did not publicly swear what they secretly abjured, but they acted under a sense of duty to the acknowledged sovereign of the kingdom, whose right to their allegiance they considered inviolable, whilst she actually occupied the throne, with the assent of the legislature and people.

Lastly, you "refer to the established maxims of human rights, on which all our patriots are accustomed to defend the American revolution." Had the signers of the Declaration of Independence publicly sworn allegiance to the British crown, and at the same time secretly protested that they did not mean to observe it, I should be at a loss how to reconcile their conduct with honor or truth. Every oath is taken in its obvious and well-known acceptation, and all devices to evade obligations which it manifestly implies, are fraudulent and criminal.

You call the protest of Cranmer a *public* act, because it was done before notaries and witnesses; but as it was done privately, whilst the oath was taken publicly before the altar, in the solemn circumstance of receiving Episcopal consecration, and as it was without the knowledge of the Pope, or his delegate, it cannot be considered otherwise than clandestine. The author of No. IV. in the Appendix to the 3d vol. of Burnet, says: "I wish it could be proved. I have two letters (MSS. Latin) of Cardinal Pole to the Archbishop Cranmer, in which he charges him with having done it only in a private manner, and brands his proceeding therein with such expressions as I am unwilling to transcribe." An oath is to be taken in the meaning of him to whom it is pledged, as expressed in the words according to their acknowledged acceptation; so that every attempt to qualify them, without the knowledge of the party interested, must necessarily be regarded as deceit aggravated by perjury.

Your justification of Cranmer's policy on divorcing the unfortunate Anne Boleyn, at the bidding of the tyrant, shows your willingness to sustain him in the discharge of his "official duty," as you designate it. Your plea for his condemnation of two heretics to death, and his exertions to obtain the signature of the young Edward to the warrant for their execution, betrays no great aversion to the intolerance of that age, the entire odium of which you would fain cast on the ancient Church, without reflecting on the glaring inconsistency of Cranmer, in condemning others to death for errors in belief, whilst he himself was engaged in the propagation of new doctrines.

Although it was notorious that he had vacillated and dissembled, he showed no indulgence to those who avowed with intrepidity their attachment to the ancient faith. The Bishops of Winchester and London, at his instigation, were cast into prison. The Bishop of Durham was deprived of his seat at the Council table. Gardiner of Winchester, having been liberated after a time, was ordered to preach by the Protector, and although he delivered the same doctrine of the Mass and Real Presence, which up to that time was professed by Cranmer and his fellow reformers, he was again thrown into prison, and detained there until the end of the reign of Edward.

It is hard to justify Cranmer for putting his signature to the death-warrant of Lord Sudely, condemned for treason on the accusation of his brother, the Protector, without the ordinary forms of trial. It had been always forbidden to ecclesiastics to concur directly to any execution, so that even under the Inquisition this was never allowed, the canonical penalty called irregularity being attached to the act. This case was further aggravated by the disregard of the usual legal forms, and by the awful circumstance that the unhappy victim was accused and condemned by his own brother.

The perjury and treason of Cranmer should not be forgotten when his claims to the title of martyr are examined. Although he avowed his conviction that by signing the instrument of Edward, by which the succession was changed, he would be guilty of both crimes, yet, after some hesitation, caused by fear of the consequences, he affixed to it his signature. When Mary challenged his obedience, he replied to her insultingly, because she was apparently unable to establish her right by force of arms. Almost the only bold act of his life, was a scurrilous publication denying that he had any share in causing the Mass to be restored in the Canterbury Cathedral after the accession of Mary to the throne. His crimes against religion were put forward at his trial, because he being an ecclesiastic they were matters of cognizance for his judges; but his treason was, no doubt, uppermost in the mind of the sovereign, as Cole, in preaching before his execution intimated, "There are other reasons which have moved the Queen and Council to order the execution of the individual present."

To eulogize a man who never in his life showed consistency even in the maintenance of error, requires much boldness as well as ingenuity, but to justify his vacillation and hypocrisy, his repeated prevarications under the fear of death, and his shameless apostacy, when all hope of escape had fled,—to proclaim such a man "a noble martyr," is, to borrow your language, outrageous effrontery. Cranmer, guilty by his own avowal of perjury and treason, as well as of heresy, was most justly consigned to a dungeon, and left there for eighteen months to reflect on his crimes, and prepare to expiate them by his death. A commission was issued to the Bishop of Gloucester, and two other ecclesiastics, to try him for being twice married whilst professing celibacy, for having denied the supremacy of the Pope, to whom he had sworn obedience, and having blasphemed the Eucharist. When found guilty, and sentenced to be degraded and executed, he signed seven successive instruments of retraction, in order to save his life. "The sixth, which was very prolix, contained an acknowledgment of all the forsaken and detested errors and superstitions of Rome, an abhorrence of his own, and a vilifying of himself, as a persecutor, a blasphemer, a mischief-maker, nay, and as the wickedest wretch that lived. And this was not all, but after they had thus humbled and mortified the miserable man with recantations and subscriptions, submissions and abjurations, putting words into his mouth which his heart abhorred; by all this drudgery they would not permit him to redeem his unhappy life, but prepared him a renunciatory oration to pronounce publicly in St. Mary's Church, immediately before he was led forth to burning."* This does not show that hope of pardon was really held out to him; but even were this the case, it could not extenuate his hypocrisy in penning documents expressing sentiments foreign from his mind. From the unsatisfactory nature of the five first retractions, it is manifest that he himself composed them, as even probably the sixth. His subscription made them all his own. At the stake he described them as "written for fear of death." He cherished hope, even when led to execution, but carried with him, concealed in his breast, a retraction of all his previous retractions, with a view to mortify and disappoint the authorities, in case mercy were not extended to him. This is the heroism which elicits your

* Strype, Eccl. Mem. vol. iv. c. 30, pp. 405–406.

applause. You, sir, who are so horror-stricken with the indulgent morality of the Jesuits, virtually adopt a foul maxim, unjustly imputed to them, and plead that "he might begin to regard his escape as a kind of duty to the truth, and thus if he could only put to sleep the suspicions of his persecutors, and gain his liberty, he might dedicate his last years to the defence and confirmation of the Gospel."* Pray, in what Gospel have you learned that evil may be done that good may come therefrom?

The example of Pope Pascal, which you allege in extenuation of Cranmer's prevarication, is not a case in point. He was suffering unjust duress from the Emperor Henry V., and at the solicitation of his friends, he compromised some of his rights, to obtain his liberty. The concessions extorted from him implied the profession of no error, although the pretensions of the Emperor to control the Church, by giving to her prelates the ensigns of ecclesiastical power, may have savored of heresy. In stating with humility the violence which he had suffered, and deploring his compromise of the rights of his office, he satisfied his duty to the Church, whilst in declining to revoke them, or to punish his oppressor by excommunication, he fulfilled abundantly the pledges which he had given. The Council of Cardinals and Bishops rightly declared that

* Vol. i. p. 308.

these forced concessions were of no avail, and smote with anathema the tyrant who wrung them from a prisoner. What resemblance does this bear to the hypocrisy of a renegade, who, when lingering in a dungeon for repeated treasons to his sovereign, feigns conversion, professes his belief in doctrines which at heart he repudiates, and when disappointed in this attempt to deceive, turns back, like a dog to the vomit, and to spite his judges, goes to the stake blaspheming the mysteries which a while before he affected to adore?

LETTER XXII.

On the Church of England.

RIGHT REVEREND SIR:

YOU have put forward very prominently the claims of the Church of England to distinct consideration, although you have carefully avoided discarding those of the various other Protestant sects, of which your Reviewers, notwithstanding their extravagant laudations, loudly complain. You, indeed, charge Dr. Milner with misrepresentation, in stating that she does not recognize their orders, on account of their want of episcopacy, and that she thus unchurches them. I scarcely deem it necessary to vindicate him on this head, further than to observe that it is notorious she does not allow them to minister without ordaining them. Whether Episcopal ordination be necessary only for the well-being of the Church, or for its mere existence, I leave you to settle with your colleagues, whose opinions are divided on this subject. Many of your ministers rebaptize persons baptized in the other sects, regarding the act as null for the want of the ministerial character; since the suppression, in 1575, of the Rubric allowing lay persons to baptize, is deemed equivalent to the statement made by Dr. Milner, that "the Church of England unanimously resolved that it could not be performed by any person but a lawful minister." You seem very desirous to stand well with the various other sects.

You are naturally anxious to establish an origin for the Church of England independent of the Roman See; but unfortunately for you, the only ancient tradition worth any notice, is that preserved by Venerable Bede, which refers it to Pope Eleutherius, in the decline of the second century. It is fair, however, to hear you: "First then, Irenæus, in A. D. 170, speaking of the unity of the faith diffused throughout the world, enumerates the Churches of Germany, the Churches among the Hibernians, and the Churches among the Celts." You take the last for Britons. Grabe, the learned Protestant editor of the works of Irenæus, understands them to have been inhabitants of Gaul, about Lyons, since the author says of himself: "We live among the Celts."* "The south and centre of France were known, even in the fifth century, by the names of Celtica and Gallia."† Our countrymen, "the Hibernians," turn out to be Iberians, inhabitants of Spain.‡ So far your researches are a failure. Nor are you more suc-

* L. 1 Adv. hær. Præf. † Mona Mission, p. 1.

‡ L. 1 Adv. hær. c. iii.

cessful in endeavoring to destroy our proofs by the testimony of Tertullian, who boasted that parts of Britain, which had been inaccessible to the Romans, had been subjected to Christ. "Britannorum inaccessa Romanis loca, Christo vero subdita." Had you reflected for a few moments, you would scarcely have put the translation in capitals, and added the observation: "There is the positive testimony, that however, or by whomsoever, the Church was first planted in Britain, which is a matter of uncertainty, *it was not planted by a missionary from Rome.*" You have strangely misunderstood your author, who contrasts the triumphs of the Gospel with the achievements of the Roman armies. He does not speak of the country whence the missionaries came. His statement, made at the close of the second or beginning of the third century, harmonizes strictly with the traditionary testimony of the English nation, recorded by Bede, concerning the conversion of the Britons under Eleutherius.

The origin of the Anglo-Saxon Church, is undeniably Roman, the fruit of the apostolic labors of the monk Augustin, and the favorite object of the solicitude of Pope Gregory. Instead of exulting in the triumph of religion by the zeal of the saintly missionary, you declare his mission "a flagrant usurpation," and insinuate that he employed force to secure success. Speaking of the refusal of the Britons to cooperate with the envoy of Gregory, you say: "Augustin left them with a menace, which the Romans convert into a prophecy. An army of the Anglo-Saxons attacked the Britons, slew twelve hundred monks, because they prayed against their enemies, and so, after a time, force compelled the British Church to submit to the authority of Rome. It was a just retribution of Providence, when the day of Reformation came, that force should break the yoke which force imposed."* The reader might suppose that Augustin or his companions had suggested these sanguinary measures, for the purpose of forcing submission. You say elsewhere, that "his (Augustin's) converts had a hand, before many years, in the cruel slaughter of twelve hundred British monks at Bangor." Yet history presents the facts in a wholly different light. The teachings of the missionaries to King Ethelbert were, "that the service of Christ ought to be voluntary, not by compulsion."† No arms but those of the Gospel were employed by them. The words of Augustin were uttered as a warning of the impending wrath of God; but his spirit had fled to rest before the sanguinary Ethelfred, King of Northumbria, listening only to his own wild hatred of the Britons, rushed on them, and slew them in great numbers. His arms made no converts. The Gospel spread by

* Vol. ii. p. 28.

† Bede, Eccl. Hist. l. i. c. xxvi.

its own mild influence. The Britons continued for a considerable time in the recesses of Wales, and it was only gradually and almost imperceptibly, that their remains were amalgamated with the Church of the Anglo-Saxons. There is no foundation for asserting that "it was accomplished by the hand of power, through Anglo-Saxon domination."*

The Church of England, at the present day, can in no sense be traced to the Britons, since Canterbury, the chief see in the new organization under Gregory, is Anglo-Saxon. The validity of her claims altogether depends on her connection with Rome through Augustin. That the succession was maintained down to Cardinal Pole is acknowledged, although the heresy and schismatical efforts of Cranmer, caused an interruption for several years. When Elizabeth came to the throne, Canterbury was vacant, and the bishops of the other sees, with the exception of Kitchin of Landaff, having refused to take the oath of supremacy, were deposed, so that all their sees were vacant. Elizabeth issued letters patent for the consecration of Matthew Parker, who is said to have been consecrated accordingly by Barlow, assisted by Scory, Coverdale, and Hodgkins, on 17th December, 1559. The fact of the consecration of Barlow himself, has never been proved from any Register, although it is

* Vol. ii. p. 35.

certain that he was elected bishop, and transferred from one see to another, under Henry VIII., and that he sat in Parliament in virtue of his office. The consecration of Parker has been denied, but it is admitted by Dr. Lingard, on the authority of the Lambeth Register. I have not time or disposition to canvass these points, which, indeed, I deem unnecessary; but as all the claims of the Church of England turn on the valid consecration of Parker, I may be allowed to state my conviction, that the form prescribed in the Ordinal of Edward VI., and alleged to have been used in his case, is altogether void and invalid. I know, Right Reverend Sir, that this is a delicate topic, on which you are scarcely disposed to enter dispassionately, deeming it enough to talk "of the utter emptiness and folly of the objection," but the impartial Thorndyke confessed that it had weight and difficulty in it.* You claim Dr. Lingard's admission in support of your orders, although he cautiously avoided any expression of opinion in regard to their validity, confining himself, as became an historian, to the statement of the fact of the ordination. With the evidence on which he relied, I am by no means satisfied; I care not to discuss it, since the examination of the Ordinal is in my opinion sufficient to decide the whole controversy.

* "Just Weights and Measures."

It is known that the personal opinion of Cranmer was, that bishops were mere officers of the crown for ecclesiastical matters; which, however, you say had no place in the system of the Church, nor in any of her standard writings. Let us examine the Ordinal, which is known to have been framed by him.

The oath of supremacy is a prominent part of it. The elect says: "I from henceforth shall utterly renounce, refuse, relinquish, and forsake the Bishop of Rome, and his authority, power, and jurisdiction. And I from henceforth, will accept, repute, and take the King's majesty to be the only supreme head in earth of the Church of England; and to my cunning, wit, and uttermost of my power, without guile, fraud, or other undue mean, I will observe, keep, maintain, and defend the whole effects and contents of all and singular acts and statutes made and to be made within this realm, in derogation, extirpation, and extinguishment of the Bishop of Rome and of his authority; and all other acts and statutes made, or to be made, in confirmation and corroboration of the King's power, of the supreme head in earth of the Church of England." This oath, which is common to all the orders, gives them a character of hostility to the divine constitution of the Church, by which bishops are subject to Peter and his successors, and of slavish subjection to the English monarch.

You remark that the elect "was presented to be consecrated Archbishop;" but this is not enough. It must be well understood and defined by the rites and prayers, what constitues a bishop, or archbishop, since the name was vague and indefinite, especially as then employed in the Church by law established. If you examine the Ordinal, you will find nothing to determine its meaning. At the end of the Litany, a prayer is said for him, "now called to the work and ministry of a bishop;" but nothing peculiar to his office is set forth. In the questions put to him, he is asked: "Are you persuaded that you be truly called to this *ministration*, according to the will of our Lord Jesus Christ, *and the order of this realm?*" Then he is questioned as to his persuasion that the "holy Scriptures contain sufficiently all doctrine required of necessity for eternal salvation," and his determination to instruct the people committed to his charge accordingly. Then the consecrating prelate asks him: "Will you . . . such as be unquiet, disobedient and criminous within your diocese, correct and punish, according to such authority as ye have by God's word, and *as to you shall be committed by the ordinance of this realm?*" Not a word occurs in all these interrogatories to mark the true office of a Christian bishop, they being on the contrary, directed to pledge the aspirant to exact conformity to the civil laws, which are stated to be a source of his authority. The prayer after the hymn is equally unsatisfactory: "Grant, we beseech Thee, to this Thy servant, such grace, that he may evermore be ready to spread abroad Thy Gospel, and glad tidings of reconcilement to God, and to use the authority given unto him, not to destroy, but to save."

The Archbishop and Bishops present lay their hands upon his head, the Archbishop saying: "Take the Holy Ghost, and remember that thou stir up the grace of God which is in thee, by imposition of hands; for God hath not given us the spirit of fear, but of power, and love, and of soberness." Nothing here occurs expressive of authority; so that in the solemn act of laying on of hands, as well as throughout the whole rite, nothing designates the office or character of bishop. It is also worthy of remark that the assistant prelates do not pronounce the words, so that if any of them were validly ordained, as was the apostate Archbishop of Spalatro, his presence would add no weight to the ceremony. Although in our ceremonial the words used in that act be simply, "Receive the Holy Ghost;" the prayer which immediately follows, determines the character of the authority, which is also expressed by the delivery of the Episcopal ring, and pastoral staff with the mitre, and other emblems of jurisdiction. All these were wanting in the ordinal of Edward.

You state that "the essence of ordination consists in the laying on of hands, and that the other rites are variable." If you mean to assert that the mere act of imposing hands is sufficient, without any words to determine the object for which it is performed, you oppose the practice and teaching of all antiquity. It has always been believed that the act must be determined by words to a definite object, since otherwise confirmation could not be distinguished from ordination. Great variety is, indeed, observable in ancient Rituals in regard to the accompanying rites; which, however, are all strongly expressive of the Episcopal authority.

I beg your attention, Right Reverend Sir, to another point of great importance, which you overlook or disregard, namely, the jurisdiction or mission necessary for the valid exercise of the powers of the episcopate. According to St. Cyprian, a bishop has no authority unless in unity, that is as one of a vast corporation spread throughout the world, and bound together in indivisible union. Separation from the body of bishops involves forfeiture of all right to exercise the powers of his office. The same father regarded the See of Rome as the centre of unity, as Hallam and Dr. Nevin acknowledge. Barlow and his assistants were not actual occupants of any see, or united with the See of Rome; they could not, therefore, communicate the governing power; so that Matthew Parker should be called, in the language of Cyprian, a stranger, an intruder, and an enemy.

Were it conceded that his ordination was valid, his occupancy of the See of Canterbury would be still an act of usurpation, contrary to all the canons of the Church. The sole sanction which can be alleged for his intrusion is the Queen's letters patent, which professed, indeed, to supply all deficiencies, but which could not bestow ecclesiastical jurisdiction.* He cannot, then, be regarded as the successor of Pole; he cannot derive under Augustin; he is the first bishop of a church establishment with royal sanction, which in the language of St. Cyprian, "is a human Church."†

From the days of Cranmer the Church of England took this earthly character, since he ascribed all his Episcopal jurisdiction to the crown, and accordingly, under Edward, it was declared by Act of Parliament that "all jurisdiction, both spiritual and temporal, was derived from the king;" and that the bishops should "thereafter be made by the King's letters patent."‡ "The intent of the contrivers," says Heylin, "was by degrees to weaken the authority of the Episcopal order, by forcing them from their stronghold of divine institution, and making them no other than the king's ministers only, his ecclesiastical sheriffs, as a man might say, to execute his will, and disperse

* See "The Validity of Anglican Ordinations and Anglican Claims to Apostolical Succession Examined, by Peter Richard Kenrick, Archbishop of St. Louis." Philadelphia, 1848.

† Ep. ad Antonian.

‡ Burnet Hist. of Ref., vol. ii. p. 69.

his mandates."* On the death of Henry, Cranmer had petitioned the young prince to be restored to his jurisdiction, and received it accordingly during the royal pleasure,† so that he is sometimes styled in his writings: "The Commissary of our dread Sovereign Lord King Edward."‡ Whilst, then, you extol his labors, and contend for his superior merit in promoting the Reformation, you should not be offended if we explain the Ordinal in conformity with his known sentiments, especially as its words are scarcely capable of any other construction. The mention made of "such authority as ye have by God's word," is too indeterminate to imply governing power derived from divine institution, and the charge delivered with the Bible sufficiently intimates that it is no more than to preach, and inculcate the contents of the divine book. The laws of the realm being acknowledged as a source of authority, the pledge to observe them is evidently directed to confine the Episcopal power within their limits.

You are offended at the remark of King James, repeated by Dr. Milner, that your service is an ill-said Mass. You know, however, that Mass continued to be said, in Latin, in the early part of Edward's reign, with an exhortation to the communicants in English, and a

* Heylin, Hist. of Ref., p. 51.

† Burnet, vol. ii. p. 9. ‡ Strype, Mem. Cranm. 202.

prayer.* It is even so styled in the first edition of the Book of Common Prayer, "The Supper of the Lord, and the Holy Communion, commonly called the Mass."† Soames avows, that the Book of Common Prayer, subsequently prepared, was "little more than a selection from the established liturgy."‡ It is true that the most important parts were in many instances omitted, and many things were inserted ill-suited to the sublime simplicity of the ancient formularies. Enough was retained to mark the original sources, and make their loss a subject of regret, whilst the additions showed the progress of the new opinions. In the ceremony of Coronation, as still performed, the ancient vestments are worn, the sacred vessels are carried to the Altar; but what constitutes the sacrifice, has disappeared, so that the solemn ceremonial turns out to be an empty pageant. Your ritual brings to my mind the ruins of the Coliseum —a grand fabric of ancient construction, supported by brick-work of modern labor.

The Book of Common Prayer was assented to by three bishops only, besides Cranmer; yet it was solemnly declared in the Act to have been made by common agreement, and "with the aid of the Holy Ghost." It was forced on

* Burnet, ii. p. 103.

† The two Liturgies of Edward VI. compared. Oxford, 1841, p. 266.

‡ Soames, iii. p. 369.

the clergy, under the heaviest pains and penalties, namely, in the first instance, the loss of their benefices, then imprisonment during a year, and in case of a third conviction imprisonment for life. Any person speaking in a disrespectful manner of it, was fined two pounds for the first offence, twenty pounds for the second offence, and for the third was subject to entire confiscation of his property and imprisonment for life.* "To make sure work of it," says Heylin, "there passed an Act. . . . for bringing in of all antiphonaries, missals, breviaries, offices, horaries, primers, and processionals, with other books of false and superstitious worship."† Yet only four years passed when Cranmer, with others, were commissioned by the young king to revise the Prayer Book, and actually expunged from it many of the chief rites retained from the old Catholic ceremonial. Chrism, heretofore used in confirmation, was henceforth omitted; extreme unction was no longer to be administered to the dying, and all mention of private confessions was avoided. The Forty-two Articles, drawn up chiefly by Cranmer, were adopted by royal authority, and passed before the public as the expression of the doctrine of the English Church. The Thirty-nine Articles, published under Elizabeth, closely resemble them. It is painful to see how the reformers

* 2 Edw. VI. 1. † Hist. of Ref. p. 78.

proceeded in the work of demolition, giving evidence of their own changes of opinion in the capricious alteration of the Liturgy. At one time they insisted that the sacrament should be received kneeling, conformably to the ancient usage, but declared that the posture should not be regarded as expressive of worship of the sacrament. The words used by us in administering it were at first retained; then others more consistent with the Calvinistic theory were substituted; then both were united. Communion under both kinds, in the second of the Six Articles of Henry VIII., was declared not necessary to salvation by the law of God. The Parliament under Edward, in 1547, ordered it to be given under both, excepting cases of sudden sickness, and other such like extremities. At one time the wafer should be round, like the Catholic host; at another, common bread was prescribed to be used in the sacrament. Oil in baptism, and prayers for the departed were first prescribed; and then forbidden, under Edward, in a few short years. The priestly ornaments were required in the first book—"a white albe, plain, with a vestment or cope;"* rejected in the second, and then restored under Elizabeth. These changes give us an idea of the narrow compass to which the magnificent ritual of the ancient Church of England is reduced.

The illustration which you give of your claims

* The Two Liturgies, p. 267.

is certainly not drawn from the Scriptures, which never represent the Church of Christ as an adulteress; still less do they sanction any usurpation of her power by rebellious children, on the plea that they are entitled to their father's inheritance. St. Paul proposes her as a model to wives, who are exhorted to obey their husbands and be subject to them, as the Church is subject to Christ. Children also are commanded to obey their parents. Nowhere is it insinuated that they should rise in revolt against their mother, accuse her of adultery, and strip her of those endowments with which Christ has enriched her. You must seek your justification elsewhere than in the divine oracles.

Your boast of the republican character of your communion ill suits its parent, the Church of England, which is purely the creature and slave of royalty. She lost her independence, when she renounced the protection of the head divinely given to the whole Church, and bowed in homage to an earthly sovereign. Accordingly, on complaint of the Parliament, of the encroachments of the convocation, Henry VIII. requested them "to forbear any more to make ordinances or constitutions, or to put them in execution, but with the royal assent and license."* No matter can be discussed by the clergy thus assembled without special leave of the Queen, or King, as the case may be; and

* See Strype, Eccl. Mem. p. 204–210.

no decision has force, unless confirmed by the Royal sanction. In the reign of Queen Anne, the Convocation condemned the writings of Whiston, as infected with Arian doctrines, and reported the condemnation to the Queen; but waited a week for her approval, which not being communicated, they broke up their meeting, and adjourned to the following year. At the opening of the next Convocation they sent a deputation to inquire into Her Majesty's gracious pleasure, in regard to the matter; but the report was ignored, and so the Convocation desisted from further action. This, I believe, is the last sign of life given by them. At present they meet for form sake, and adjourn.

The appointment of Bishops in the Church of England is a purely royal or ministerial transaction. When the fortunate individual has been fixed on who is to enjoy the vast revenues of some diocese, with the title of Bishop, the Royal *congé d'elire* issues, directed to the Dean and Chapter, requiring them within a certain number of days, to proceed to the election of a fit and worthy person to fill the vacant See, accompanied by *letters missive*, recommending and enjoining them to choose a certain individual. Any delay to exercise their elective privilege in favor of the individual recommended, is punishable with imprisonment.

Nous avons changé tout cela. So you may boast of the republican character of your Church discipline. Your titles are not taken from the cities in which you reside, as was the practice of the Church in ancient times, and as is still the custom in England and in Catholic countries, but from the territory, over which you claim jurisdiction. The control of an Archbishop is removed, and precedency with a few privileges, is allowed to the senior Bishop, so that authority shifts her quarters, according to accidental priority of ordination; the Bishops are elected by Diocesan Conventions, in which the laity are represented. These annual conventions regulate the local affairs of each diocese, and appoint standing committees of clergy and laymen to assist the Bishop in the chief management of the diocese, or to control him. The vestries of each parish, elected by the congregation, choose the Rector, who is instituted by the Bishop at their instance. Triennial Conventions of the same mixed character, regulate the general interests of your religious denomination. This, I presume, is a fair outline of your Church government. That it is far more republican than the government of the Church of England is very manifest. How far it is advantageous to the freedom of clerical action, and the just influence of the ministry, you can better tell, who some years ago lamented that the episcopal and pastoral relation is but the shadow of what it once was. Many of your clergy regard it as only a decent kind of Congregationalism, with the forms of episcopacy. The Rectors are practically independent of the Bishop, whose authority is reduced to the mere performance of certain official acts, with little room for the exercise of his conscientious judgment. Hence he is forced to forbear, whilst some evangelical clergyman fraternizes with the sects, or resists his claims to the exercise of some sacred office in a Church of his own Diocese. This independence, although in accordance with our civil polity, does not exhibit unity and order, such as we should expect to find in the Church of God. The delivery of the keys of the Church by the Senior Warden to the Rector, in the ceremony of institution, though intended as a mere recognition of his office, is a practical indication that its exercise is to a great extent, dependent on the good-will of the congregation. As the system is your own, you deserve to enjoy whatever popularity is attached to it, whilst you experience its inconveniences and disadvantages. In the exercise of holy functions, the priest should act and be regarded as the messenger of the God of hosts, the minister of Christ, and dispenser of Divine mysteries. In order to be useful to the faithful, he should be free from their control, and subject only to the direction and authority of his ecclesiastical superior. Whatever disturbs this order, frustrates his ministrations, and reduces religion to the level of earthly things.

LETTER XXIII.

On the Catholic Church.

Right Reverend Sir:

YOUR attack on the Catholic Church, as corrupt and idolatrous, is qualified by the admission that she is, nevertheless, a true and real Church, because she retains the great mysteries of Christian faith, and the ministry instituted by Christ. The comparison of an adulteress, who is nevertheless a real wife, is employed by you to illustrate this position. In truth you could not reject her altogether, without abandoning all the claims of your own communion. The Holy Scriptures and the fathers, in speaking of the Church, declare her to be the object of the special love of Christ, and a model of entire fidelity and obedience, whom Christian wives should imitate: "As the Church is subject to Christ, so also let wives be subject to their husbands in all things."* If, with St. Augustin, we are to understand the Apostle as speaking of the Church triumphant, when he describes her as glorious, not having spot, or wrinkle, or any such thing, we must at least recognize her as free from all idolatry or super-

* Eph. vi. 24.

stition in her solemn worship, and from all error in her teaching, since God would not otherwise dwell in her as in his chosen temple, nor would she be "the house of the living God, the pillar and the ground of truth." If not only scandals from time to time spring up in her borders, but depraved principles spread their poison, then in no sense have the promises of Christ a meaning, since the gates of hell have prevailed against her. We must either disbelieve His words, or maintain that the Church, despite of scandals, has always been faithful to her mission, which is to proclaim revealed truth, and furnish men with means of sanctification.

The continuance of the Church is a standing miracle of Divine Providence, which attests the divinity of our Lord in a manner more striking than any other proof which can be furnished. It is the fulfilment, under our eyes, of the splendid prophecy made by Himself, conformably to the predictions of Daniel, David, and Isaiah, and under circumstances which forbade any human hope of a favorable issue. He foretold that His Church should be spread throughout all nations, and persecuted and oppressed, but never wholly vanquished. The opposition of the Jews and heathens threatened her with speedy ruin, but at the opening of the fourth century, after the sacrifice of millions of her children, she received the homage of the successor of the Cæsars. Heresy, in all its endless forms, subsequently assailed her, and emperors and kings used their power to corrupt her faith, and restrict her action, but she guarded the deposit of divine truth with unfailing watchfulness, and cast from her the bonds that were thrown around her. The jealousies of nations have constantly obstructed her progress, and disturbed her tranquillity, sometimes despoiling her of her possessions, and often loading her with chains, yet she advances, diffusing blessings in her pathway, and confounding her enemies by her achievements. You object to her success in missionary enterprises being taken as a test of her truth, although you should reflect that the speedy propagation of Christianity is among the most brilliant evidences of the truth of the Gospel. But be it as you say, "The results of two or three hundred years are not to be taken as the measure of fulfilment" of the Gospel promises. The permanence of the Church, now more than eighteen centuries, must count for something in estimating her claims to be regarded as the messenger of God to men. How has she contrived to maintain herself, whilst so much corruption, as you allege, was preying on her vitals, and so much violence assailed her from without? "Often have they fought against me from my youth; let Israel now say: Often have they fought against me from my youth; for they could not *prevail* over me."* The infidel beholds the phenomenon, and is utterly amazed; the sectary views it

* Ps. cxxviii.

and blasphemes. One calls this wonderful institution a master-piece of human policy; the other styles it a grand device of Satan; but there it stands triumphant over every opposition. You may well despair of overthrowing it, and avow that it will subsist until the second coming of our Saviour; but you should reflect that were it a corrupt institution, with a merely human basis, it could not possibly survive the attacks made on it so incessantly. You should then give glory to Christ our Lord for His mercy to mankind in securing the transmission of revealed truth by the Church, notwithstanding the unworthiness of many of her children, and in affording us means of sanctification, wholly independent of the personal merits of the officers commissioned to impart them.

I am surprised, Sir, that you should deny that the Church is any longer Catholic in the sense in which it was proclaimed by St. Augustin, namely, as a united body spread throughout the world. "Here is a test," you say, "which was conclusive in the days of Augustin, but which ceased to be so ever since the ambition of Rome separated the Eastern from the Western churches, in the ninth century." Is this, then, the mark and attribute of the Church assigned in all the ancient creeds, which are still repeated as words of divine faith? In your public ministrations you say: "I believe in the Holy Catholic Church." You write, the Church for nearly a thousand years has ceased to be Catholic. The

Donatists spoke to the same effect, to whom St. Augustin replied: "All nations have believed in Christ. But that Church which consisted of all nations is now no more, it has perished. This is said by those who are not in it. O! shameless assertion. Does the Church no longer exist, because you are not in it? Take care lest you be no more; for she shall be, although you be not. The spirit of God foresaw this language, which is abominable, detestable, full of presumption and falsehood, void of all semblance of truth, illumined with no ray of wisdom, seasoned with no wit, vain, rash, reckless, destructive, and He spoke, 'as it were, against them, in announcing unity, when the people assembled together, and kings, to serve the Lord.' 'Declare unto me the fewness of my days.' What does this mean? How did he declare it? 'Behold I am with you to the consummation of the world.'"*

You quote St. Isidore, of Seville, as explaining the term Catholic in a variety of ways, by which you wish to insinuate that its obvious and direct meaning, which implies general diffusion, need not be insisted on; but can you honestly maintain that such is the scope of the author? "The Church," he says, "is strictly so styled (*Ecclesia*) because she calls all to her and gathers them together. And she is called *Catholic*, because she is *established* throughout the world." The

* In Ps. ci. Enarr. Serm. II. n. 8. vol. iv. col. 1105.

Latin term *instituta*, as here applied, has evidently this force. What he adds, is not to weaken or render doubtful this explanation, but to show that besides this general diffusion, she is also Catholic in the universal character of her teaching, which regards heavenly and earthly things, and is addressed to men of all classes, and intended to remedy all the moral disorders of mankind.*

You strive to substitute another view for that of Catholic diffusion. You appeal to that "which the Catholic Church has universally taught from days of old, that which has been believed everywhere, always, by all." Tried by this standard, you will be found wanting. Compare, if you will, the Thirty-nine Articles with the general teaching of antiquity, and you will be forced to acknowledge the vast discrepancy.

The unity of the Catholic Church in all defined doctrines is a striking fact, which every one knows and feels. In order to verify it, it is not necessary, as you insinuate, to ask every individual Catholic his faith; you can take any one, even a child who has learned his catechism, and satisfy yourself. The books of instruction published in various countries, the sermons preached, the worship offered up, all attest it in a manner not easy to be mistaken. Your kindliness acknowledges it after this fashion: "We doubt not that there is quite as much of this sort

* De Offic. Eccl l. 1. c. 1.

of unity among the Budhist and the Hindoo idolaters, and the followers of the false prophet." The freedom of opinion on all matters not of faith, is no wise inconsistent with this strict unity. But the Church of England cannot justly lay claim to it, whilst the collision of views in regard to the Thirty-nine Articles, is notorious.

To illustrate the mark of holiness, Dr. Milner pointed, among other things, to the various orders which are devoted to works of charity and mercy. You deny the Church all merit in this respect, because they originated from the zeal of individuals, and not from any decree of Councils or Popes, and "they may spring up in any other church and receive its sanction, without touching a single point in controversy belonging to the Reformation." Individuals could effect but little, were it not for the sanction and guidance of authority, which gives a direction and blessing to their labors. Protestants have from time to time tried to rival these benevolent institutions, with little success, precisely because the soil was not congenial. Dr. Nevin, avows this distinctly: "Such an institution as that of the Sisters of Charity, can never be transferred to purely Protestant ground; as no such ground either could ever have given it birth. Attempts are made in our own time to furnish a Protestant version of the same idea, under what claims to be a higher and more evangelical form; for the purpose of supplying an evident want. But nothing of this sort will ever equal the original design, or be more indeed than a weak and stunted copy of this on the most narrow and ephemeral scale. It is only in the bosom of ideas, principles, and associations, which are Catholic distinctively, and not Protestant, that charity of this sort finds itself perfectly at home. And just so it is with the piety of this Church in general. It is fairly and truly native to the soil from which it springs. That Church, with all its supposed errors and sins, has ever had power in its own way to produce a large amount of very lovely religion. If it has been the mother of abominations, it has been unquestionably the mother also of martyrs and saints. It is a sorry business to pretend to deny this, or to try to falsify the fact into the smallest possible dimensions."*

The argument of Dr. Milner in favor of the Church, derived from the miracles which attest the sanctity of her children, does not interfere with her claims to obedience in virtue of her Divine commission. She produces this as a voucher for her authority altogether sufficient. Yet those wonders, which from time to time happen through the prayers of holy men, serve to confirm faith, and show forth the Divine attributes. The passage which you quote from St. Gregory the Great, recognizes the principle of Church authority as independent of miracles,

* Mercersburg Review, September, 1851. Art. Early Christianity.

so that if any one should perform them in opposition to the Church, they should be disregarded as tainted with pride, and hateful to Him, who at the last day will reject some wonder-workers as doers of iniquity. This is a safe criterion, by which we may distinguish the false wonders of Satan from works truly Divine. But when extraordinary works are performed in support of revealed truth, and for ends every way worthy of God, their Divine character being thus manifest, new lustre is added thereby to faith, and the Church receives from them support, not indeed necessary to substantiate her claims, but highly serviceable to confirm the weak in faith, and to confound unbelievers. That St. Gregory so regarded them is evident from his Dialogues in which he records them. I must award you the praise of ingenuity, in availing yourself of the strongest passages that have been uttered against heresy, to weaken the evidences which support the Church. St. Gregory says: "The Holy Church disregards the miracles of heretics, if they perform any, because she does not recognize them as an evidence of holiness. For the proof of holiness is not to work miracles, but to love others as ourselves, and to entertain correct sentiments in regard to God, and to think better of our neighbor than ourselves. .... The gift of brotherly love is, therefore, a token that we are disciples of Christ. Which love all heretics abjure, by separating from the unity of the universal Church. .... Without doubt the Holy Church considers all heretics unworthy of eternal life, because in the name of Christ they war on the name of Christ."* Elsewhere he says of miracles in general: "Those corporal wonders sometimes manifest holiness; but they do not constitute it."†

You call St. Isidore, of Seville, to your assistance, as if he undervalued miracles, and foretold that the Church would be utterly destitute of their support. He follows closely on the footsteps of St. Gregory,‡ who indeed avowed that miracles were not now as frequent in the Church as at its commencement, but distinctly recorded many which had come to his knowledge. St. Isidore says, that the world was won to the faith by the miracles of the Apostles, but that the faithful are now to shed abroad the light of good works as the fruits of their faith. He does not deny, that miracles were occasionally performed in his own time, which, on the contrary, he intimates by observing that "miracles and virtues will cease from the Church before the appearance of Antichrist." By virtues, "*virtutes*," he seems to understand miracles according to the *Scriptural* force of the corresponding Greek term, so that the same idea is expressed in a twofold manner; for he states that the cessation of these gifts will afford occasion to the manifestation of the patience of the saints, and the inconstancy of the reprobate

* Mor. L. xx. in cap. xxx. B. Job. † Hom. xxix. in Ev. Marci.
‡ L. xxvii.; Mor. c. xviii.

who will fall away, and to fiercer persecution on the part of the enemies of the Church.*

I shall take no pains to claim for the Church a republican character, because she is a Divine institution, deriving her authority from above, and directed to lead men to eternal happiness. We are not at liberty to model her according to our political predilections, or to suit the popular fancy. She is, if you will, a monarchy, since she has one supreme ruler, representing Christ, her Divine Founder; but the caprice, or will, of no individual can change her doctrines, or maxims; no authority of an arbitrary character can be claimed in the name of Him, the sceptre of whose kingdom is a sceptre of justice. The bishops, governing their respective flocks throughout the world, share with their head the solicitude with which he is specially charged, and feed the sheep of Christ, not lording it over them, but becoming their model from the heart. The priests are their fellow-laborers, discharging the duties of their office under their authority and guidance. The faithful generally, without distinction of castes, or classes, are the objects of the tender care of the pastors of the Church, who watch incessantly as being to render an account for their souls. Those who will examine closely the features of the Church, according to her divine constitution, will find enough to satisfy them that she is not anti-republican. The common good of all, is her great object; her offices are open to

* L. iii.; Sentent. c. xxvii.

all, to the man of humble birth, as well as to the nobleman; her power is limited by truth and justice. As regards political institutions, she is wholly independent of any, and suited to all. It is not her province to model or fashion them; but being indifferent to each particular form of social organization, she studies only to infuse the spirit and maxims of Christ, and thus to modify and mitigate whatever may be exorbitant and unjust. "The Christian religion," says St. Priest, "which has existed for near two thousand years, is not indissolubly attached to any political form. Under the shadow of absolute thrones, or of limited monarchies,—on the borders of the republican lake of William Tell, in America, which is still more republican, it flourishes as an imperishable plant, nourished by the juices of earth, and refreshed by the waters of heaven. It is not a local, but a universal religion."*

I remain, Right Reverend Sir,

Your obedient servant,

FRANCIS PATRICK KENRICK,

Archbishop of Baltimore.

BALTIMORE, May 1, 1855.

* Histoire de la Royauté par le Comté Alexis de Saint Priest. l. ii. p. 92.

www.ingramcontent.com/pod-product-compliance
Lightning Source LLC
LaVergne TN
LVHW020210110826
845151LV00003B/663
9781425534745